A Wine & Food Affair

Tasting Along the Wine Road
COOKBOOK

A COLLECTION OF RECIPES FROM
"A Wine & Food Affair"

COOKBOOK VOLUME 14

Recipes from the Wineries and Lodgings of the
Alexander, Dry Creek and Russian River Valleys.

WINE ROAD
NORTHERN SONOMA COUNTY

A custom cookbook published by

Wine Road Northern Sonoma County

P.O. Box 46, Healdsburg, CA 95448

wineroad.com

Content © Wine Road Northern Sonoma County

Design © Pembroke Studios, pembrokestudios.com

Illustrations © Chris Witkowski, chriswitkowski.com

Lodging and Winery photos © Lenny Siegel, siegelphotographic.com

Bottle Shots © Kelly McManus, kellymcmanusphotography.com

Editor © Linda Murphy

ISBN 978-1-4675-3056-953000

Printed in China

TABLE OF CONTENTS

A.   FOREWORD

1.   BRUNCH

3.   Applewood's White Gazpacho
5.   Eggs Florentine with Hollandaise Sauce
7.   Spinach Fritatta
9.   Cheese Soufflés
11.   Italian Brunch Asparagus
13.   Baked Pears with Granola
15.   Roasted Pepper & Pea Tortilla
17.   Crispy Pork Belly Sandwich
19.   Potato, Cheddar & Mushroom Egg Bake
21.   Pumpkin Waffles with Apple Cider Sauce
23.   Maple & Fruit Bread
25.   Oatmeal-Blueberry Pancakes
27.   Melon Delight with Honey-Lime Sauce
29.   Orange-Bittersweet Chocolate Muffins
31.   Santa Fe Bake with Sun-Dried Tomato Sauce
33.   Baked Cheese Omelet
35.   Orange Cream-Filled French Toast with Orange Sauce
37.   Nut-Crusted French Toast
39.   Morning Glorious Muffins
41.   Aunt Wanda's Okie Doughs
43.   Mexican Cornbread
45.   Potato & Asparagus Tart
47.   Mushroom Bisque
49.   Spinach Fritatta
51.   Liberty Duck Confit Hash Cakes
53.   Spicy Scrambled Eggs

55.   APPETIZERS

57.   Duck Chilaquiles with Cherry-Guajillo Chile Sauce
59.   Alligator Sausage Cheesecake with Shrimp
61.   Dungeness Crab Salad
63.   Spicy Crab Arancini
65.   Arancini di Riso
67.   Kathleen's Sweet & Spicy Grilled Prawns
69.   Point Reyes Blue Cheese Paté
71.   Zinfandel-Braised Pork with Vella Dry Jack Polenta

TABLE OF CONTENTS

73. Red, Smoked & Blue Filet Mignon
75. Bruschetta with Mushroom Pesto
77. Wood Stove Fondue with Tri-Color Potatoes
79. Costeaux French Bakery Focaccia
81. Swedish Gravlax with Mustard Sauce

83. SOUPS

85. Pumpkin Red Curry
87. Harvest Ribollita
89. Honey Harvest Tomato Bisque
91. Soupe au Pistou
93. Chris Hanna's Autumn Corn Chowder
95. PAG Soup
97. Roasted Apple & Butternut Squash Bisque
99. Zin-Marinated Pork & Apple Chili
101. Chanterelle Soup with Turkey & Cranberry Garnish
103. Posole
105. Mushroom & Brie Soup with Truffle Oil
107. Mushroom-Leek Zuppa

109. SALADS & SIDES

111. Rouge et Noir Brie Quiche
113. Seared Pork Tenderloin with Rocket-Chicory Salad
115. 'Baked Comfort' Tomato Bread Pudding

117. PASTA & RICE

119. Risotto Amista
121. Baked Rigatoni with Olives & Sausage
123. Spaghetti with Meat Sauce
125. Risotto with Roasted Cippolini, Portobellos & Rainbow Chard
127. Spring Hill Mac & Cheese with Bacon
129. Lemon Risotto
131. Mushroom Ragout
133. Cannelloni con Spinaci e Salmone
135. Peppery Pancetta Pasta
137. Risotto al Radicchio Rosso
139. Bill's Bolognese
141. Diane's Baked Penne Pasta

TABLE OF CONTENTS

143. ENTRÉES

145. Chicken Ragout with Soft Polenta
147. Sausage & Mushroom Ragout
149. French Dip Sliders with Karma Au Jus
151. Mom's Sunday Sauce with Sausages & Meatballs
153. Spiedini d' Loiodice con Polenta Enrico
155. Pollo a la Catalana
157. Roasted Pork Shoulder with Dried Cherry, Bacon & Sweet Onion Compote
159. Moroccan Lamb Stew with Tart Cherries
161. Rustic Restaurant Marrakesh Lamb
163. Zin-Braised Beef
165. St. George & Bacon Grilled Cheese with Caramelized Onions & Herb Aioli
167. Sicilian Lamb Meatballs
169. Not So Traditional Osso Buco with Gremolata
171. Lip-Smackin' Baby Back Ribs
173. Chicken Marbella
175. Cuban Pork Stew with Sweet Potato Mash
177. Red Wine-Braised Short Ribs with Truffled Celery Root Puree
179. Kobe Tri-Tip Sandwiches with Cabernet-Braised Cabbage & Blue Cheese-Buttermilk Dressing
181. Osso Buco Stew with Gremolata & Freeze-Dried Corn
183. Sausage Skewers with Mushrooms and Syrah Dipping Sauce
185. Coq au Vin
187. Wild Boar Sausage
189. Oxtail & Short Rib Ragu over Soft Polenta
191. Soul Surfer Ribs
193. It's Just Pork ... and Chutney
195. Turkey & White Bean Chili
197. New Contadina
199. Wild Game Stew
201. Duck & Pork Cassoulet
203. Beef Ribs with Zinfandel-Maple Reduction Sauce
205. Josh Silvers' Drunken Duck
207. Nonna's Italian Meatballs
209. Roast Duck Bread Pudding
211. Duck Confit with Emily's Cuvée Reduction & Creamy Polenta
213. Meatloaf with Pancetta & Shiitake Mushrooms
215. Pork & Pancetta Pot Pie
217. Chicken & Sausage Jambalaya
219. Ricotta Malfatti with Sweet Italian Sausage, Spinach & Peppers

TABLE OF CONTENTS

221. Margherita Pizza
223. South African-Style Boerewors Sausages with Merlot-Caramelized Onions
225. Braised Pork Shank with Apricots
227. Spinach & Portobello Mushroom Lasagne
229. Provencal Lamb Daube with Red Wine, Olives & Oranges
231. Steak Sapphire with Sautéed Spinach, Crab & Béarnaise Sauce
233. Creole Lobster
235. Petite Ribs & Celariac Puree
237. Frane's Mom's Bakalar
239. Sriracha Chicken
241. Smokin' Pulled Pork Sliders with Cider Vinegar Sauce
243. Kissable Baked Polenta with Pinot Noir-Braised Wild Mushrooms
245. Cabernet-Braised Short Ribs
247. Rockin' Rattler Pork & Beef Sugo over Polenta
249. Mesquite-Charred Bistro Steak with Zinfandel Reduction & Pilaf
251. Grilled Skirt Steak with Chimi Sauce
253. Korean-Style Braised Short Rib Rice Bowl with Kimchi

255. **DESSERTS**
257. Panettone
259. Dark Chocolate Dreams with Cranberry Relish
261. Devil's Zin Cake
263. Chocolate Cupcakes with Salted Caramel Frosting & Red Wine Drizzle
265. Chocolate-Dipped Pistachio Biscotto with Artisan Salt
267. Chocolate Ganache Cupcakes
269. Smoky Autumn & Bacon Truffles

271. **Recipe Index by Winery & Lodging**
275. **Thank You**
276. **What's New**
277. **Annual Wine Road Events**
278. **Feel-Good Moment**
279. **Our AVAs (American Viticultural Areas)**

FOREWORD
Jeff Mall

proprietor, chef and farmer, Zin Restaurant & Wine Bar, Healdsburg, CA

The first time I can remember visiting Sonoma County was when I was a kid in the early 1980s. My family drove to Petaluma to pick up two baby lambs for my brother's 4-H project. Even as a young boy, I was taken by the rolling green hills and farms of the area. Growing up in a Central Valley farming family, farms, ranches and livestock were nothing new, but along the winding back roads of Sonoma County, things were different. Everything seemed smaller, slower and more picturesque.

I knew I wanted to be a chef.

Choosing a career in the kitchen meant not following the family path in farming. Yet even back then, I knew that my background in agriculture would be a part of my culinary future. Growing the food I would cook just seemed natural.

Fast forward 30 years and I'm back in Sonoma County, and in one of the few places in the world where one can be a farmer and a chef. As a chef, I am constantly reminded of how lucky I am to be in a place with so many local and diverse culinary resources. Sonoma County is the market basket for top restaurants and stores around the country. They pour our wines and olive oils, serve our cheeses, showcase our meats and poultry, and order overnight delivery of our produce and seafood to their back doors.

As a farmer, I understand why and how all of this comes together. Not only do we have the perfect climate to grow a variety of crops, but we also have people who have dedicated their lives to their craft. It is this dedication to growing the best grapes, raising the best lamb and crafting the best cheeses that puts us ahead of the rest of the country when it comes to being a food and wine destination.

I love designing menus for Zin that showcase not just our cooking style, but also our farming.

Eggs from our chickens, honey from our bees and produce we grow from seed all have starring roles in the restaurant at different times of the year. But Zin isn't alone in bringing you the best of what Sonomans can grow, raise and craft. Many Sonoma County chefs embrace this lifestyle, and we are all happy to share it with you.

Cheers!

RECIPES

from the wineries & lodgings

BRUNCH

Applewood's White Gazpacho

Eggs Florentine with Hollandaise Sauce

Spinach Fritatta

Cheese Soufflés

Italian Brunch Asparagus

Roasted Pepper & Pea Tortilla

Baked Pears with Granola

Crispy Pork Belly Sandwich

Potato, Cheddar & Mushroom Egg Bake

Pumpkin Waffles with Apple Cider Sauce

Maple & Fruit Bread

Oatmeal-Blueberry Pancakes

Melon Delight with Honey-Lime Sauce

Orange-Bittersweet Chocolate Muffins

Santa Fe Bake with Sun-Dried Tomato Sauce

Baked Cheese Omelet

Orange Cream-Filled French Toast with Orange Sauce

Nut-Crusted French Toast

Morning Glorious Muffins

Aunt Wanda's Okie Doughs

Mexican Cornbread

Potato & Asparagus Tart

Mushroom Bisque

Spinach Fritatta

Liberty Duck Confit Hash Cakes

Spicy Scrambled Eggs

APPLEWOOD INN & RESTAURANT

The best part of this recipe is its versatility. Don't like honeydew? Try cantaloupe or galia melon. Want something with more zing? Add a jalapeño. If the melon isn't quite ripe enough, more honey will sweeten it up nicely. Allergic to almonds? Unseasoned bread crumbs will give this chilled soup its body.

13555 Highway 116
Guerneville, CA 95446
707-869-9093
applewoodinn.com

applewood's

WHITE GAZPACHO

vegi

chef Shelley Cerneant

SERVES 6-8

½ cup blanched almonds
¾ cup ice
1 cup water
1 clove garlic
1 tablespoon Sherry vinegar
2 tablespoons honey
1 honeydew melon, seeds
   and rind removed, cut into
   pieces
1 cucumber, seeds and skin
   removed, cut into pieces
salt to taste
extra-virgin olive oil to taste

In a blender or food processor, blend the first 6 ingredients until they're very smooth. Add the melon and cucumber, one handful at a time, until they're well blended and smooth. Strain into a large bowl.

Refrigerate the gazpacho until it's well-chilled. Before serving, drizzle the surface of the soup with extra virgin olive oil.

AVALON LUXURY BED & BREAKFAST

This is a great meatless alternative to the classic Eggs Benedict. If you have gluten-intolerant diners, you can substitute cooked rice, quinoa or another grain for the bread crumbs. The hollandaise sauce recipe is so quick and easy, you'll be making it all the time. Just make sure your gym membership is up to date!

11910 Graton Road
Sebastopol, CA 95472
707-824-0880
avalonluxuryinn.com

EGGS FLORENTINE
with hollandaise sauce

chef Hilary McCalla

vegi

SERVES 6

EGGS

⅓ cup pine nuts

1 red bell pepper

1-½ cups coarse bread
   crumbs

12 cups fresh spinach leaves

½ small red onion

splash of olive oil

12 eggs

salt and pepper to taste

HOLLANDAISE SAUCE

3 egg yolks

1 tablespoon fresh lemon
   juice

1 teaspoon Dijon mustard

1 cup salted butter

To prepare the eggs, toast the pine nuts in a small skillet and set them aside to cool. Julienne the red bell pepper and cut the strips into confetti-size pieces. Sprinkle 1/4 cup bread crumbs on each of 6 dinner plates. Chop the spinach. Finely chop the onion.

Heat the olive oil in a large skillet. Over medium heat, sauté the onions until they're translucent. Add the spinach and cook until the spinach softens, adding salt and pepper to taste.

Poach the eggs until the whites are set – about 4 minutes. Place a small scoop of the cooked spinach mixture over the bread crumbs on each plate. With the back of a spoon, make two little wells in the spinach to receive the eggs.

While the eggs cook, prepare the hollandaise sauce. Separate the eggs and reserve the whites for another purpose. In a blender, place the egg yolks, lemon juice and mustard. Heat the butter in a small saucepan to piping hot, but do not brown it. Turn on the blender and with the blades running, slowly add the hot butter. Place a tea towel atop the blender to catch any splatters. Whirl until the sauce is just thickened; do not over mix, or the sauce will become too thick to pour.

To serve, gently place a poached egg in each of the two wells in the spinach. Top the eggs with hollandaise sauce and a sprinkling of red bell pepper and toasted pine nuts.

BELLA VILLA MESSINA

We serve our delicious fritatta each morning to groups headed out for a full day of wine tasting. It's a great base protein to get you ready and fueled for the rest of the day!

316 Burgundy Road
Healdsburg, CA 95448
707-433-6655
bellavillamessina.com

SPINACH FRITATTA

vegi

chef Jerry Messina

SERVES 10-12

½ large bag washed spinach

18 eggs

1 16-ounce tub cottage
   cheese

1 cup Parmesan cheese,
   grated

Preheat oven to 350°.

Place the spinach in a microwave-safe dish and microwave on medium-high for approximately 4 minutes, until the leaves are wilted.

Apply a film of nonstick spray to a baking dish and spread the wilted spinach in the bottom of the dish.

In a large bowl, whisk the eggs and blend in the cottage and Parmesan cheeses. Pour the mixture over the spinach and bake in the oven for approximately 1 hour, until the top of the frittata is golden and is firm to the touch. It will hold in the oven on the "warm" setting.

As an option, add finely chopped mushrooms and yellow onions while whisking the eggs.

BELLE DE JOUR INN

We serve this dish at many of our breakfasts, accompanied by shallot-butter toast and fresh fruit of the season.

16276 Healdsburg Avenue
Healdsburg, CA 95448
707-431-9777
belledujourinn.com

CHEESE SOUFFLÉS

vegi

chef Brenda Hearn

SERVES 6

4 eggs, separated
2 ounces butter
⅓ cup all-purpose flour
2 cups milk
½ cup mature Cheddar
   cheese, grated
½ cup smoked Gouda
   cheese, grated

Preheat oven to 400°.

In a mixing bowl, beat the egg whites until soft peaks form, and set the bowl aside. In a separate bowl, stir the egg yolks and set them aside.

Place the butter in a saucepan over low heat and stir until it's melted. Add the flour and cook for 1 minute, stirring constantly. Remove the pan from the heat and gradually whisk in the milk, making sure there are no lumps.

Return the pan to the heat and stir constantly until the mixture boils and thickens. Remove it from the heat and stir in the cheeses and egg yolks.

Fold the beaten egg whites into the cheese mixture. Pour into 6-ounce ramekins.

Bake for approximately 25 minutes, or until the soufflés are puffed and golden brown. Serve immediately.

CAMELLIA INN

Owner Lucy Lewand says: "This is a yummy brunch dish that my niece Nichelle Passanisi brought to our family Easter brunch. Nichelle once worked at the inn as an innkeeper and was great in the kitchen. We all loved the combination of salty, sweet, creamy and tart in her dish. My father grows many of the fresh vegetables we use in our seasonal garden-to-guest breakfasts, and asparagus is a favorite."

211 North Street
Healdsburg, CA 95448
707-433-8182
camelliainn.com

italian brunch
ASPARAGUS

brought to our family by Nichelle Passanisi

SERVES 8

2 ounces thinly sliced
   prosciutto
1 pound asparagus spears
2 teaspoons extra-virgin olive
   oil, plus 2 tablespoons
kosher salt and freshly
   ground pepper
2 tablespoons fresh
   lemon juice
1/4 small melon (about 12
   ounces) peeled, seeded
   and cut into 3/4-inch cubes
4 ounces fresh mozzarella or
   burrata cheese, cut into
   3/4-inch cubes
2 tablespoons pine nuts,
   toasted (see note)

Place an oven rack in the center of the oven. Preheat oven to 350°. Using the broiler is fine, too.

Line a baking sheet with parchment paper. Place the prosciutto slices in a single layer on the parchment. Bake for 12 to 14 minutes until the prosciutto is crispy. Transfer to paper towels to drain. Chop the prosciutto into 1/4-inch pieces.

Place a grill pan over medium-high heat or preheat a gas or charcoal grill. In a medium bowl, toss together the asparagus and 2 teaspoons of olive oil. Season with salt and pepper. Grill the spears for 2 to 3 minutes on each side, until they're crisp-tender.

In a medium bowl, combine the lemon juice and 2 tablespoons of olive oil. Whisk until they're combined, and season with salt and pepper to taste. Add the melon and cheese, and toss until all ingredients are combined. Arrange the asparagus on a platter. Using a slotted spoon, place the melon and cheese on top of the asparagus. Drizzle any remaining vinaigrette over the top. Sprinkle the prosciutto and pine nuts on top and serve.

Note: To toast pine nuts, arrange them in a single layer on a baking sheet. Bake in a preheated 350° oven for 8 to 12 minutes, until they're lightly browned.

CASE RANCH INN

We have served this dish for the decade we have been in business. Our guests love the flavor combinations, and it seems to work well with any variety of pear that is in season. This recipe also works well with crispy apple varieties.

7446 Poplar Drive
Forestville, CA 95436
877-887-8711
caseranchinn.com

BAKED PEARS
with granola

vegi

chef Diana Van Ry

SERVES 8-10

4 ripe d'anjou pears, or any
   others in season
1/2 cup granola
1/4 cup orange juice
2 tablespoons butter, melted
ground cinnamon
ground nutmeg
ground cloves
1 6-ounce container vanilla
   yogurt
mint sprigs, for garnish

Preheat oven to 350°.

Slice the pears in half, removing the cores and stems. Evenly spread the granola in the bottom of a glass baking dish. Place the pears cut side down on top of the granola. Pour the orange juice over the pears and evenly distribute the melted butter over each pear. Sprinkle lightly with cinnamon and nutmeg, and then add a pinch of cloves to each pear.

Bake for approximately 30 minutes, or until the pears are tender. Pierce each one gently with a fork to test for firmness.

To serve, place each pear in a small bowl and top with a teaspoon of yogurt and a sprig of mint.

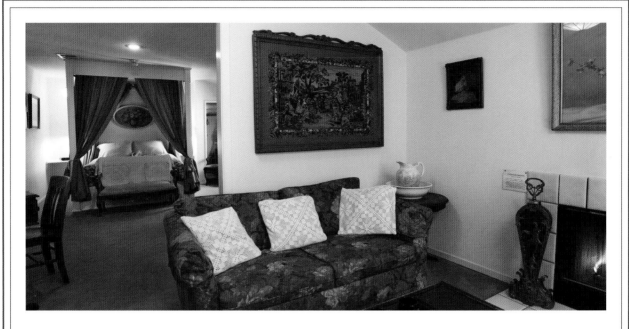

CREEKSIDE INN & RESORT

This dish has a great smoky aroma and flavor that comes from roasted red bell peppers. I recommend roasting the peppers on a gas burner until they're black. Gently wipe the char off the peppers – do not rinse them. We like to serve the tortilla with melon slices.

16180 Neeley Road
Guerneville, CA 95446
800-776-6586
creeksideinn.com

roasted pepper & pea
TORTILLA

chef Mark Crescione

vegi

SERVES 6

⅓ cup olive oil
1 large white onion, chopped
4 Yukon Gold potatoes,
　peeled and sliced
　⅛-inch thick
8 large eggs
2 red bell peppers, roasted,
　cored, peeled and cut into
　small pieces
½ cup frozen peas
1 to 1-½ teaspoons salt
¼ teaspoon black pepper

In a large bowl, mix half of the oil with the onion, potatoes, half of the salt and all of the pepper, coating the vegetables. Heat half of the remaining oil in a 10-inch nonstick sauté pan and add the onion-potato mixture. Cover the pan and cook on the stovetop for about 30 minutes, stirring every 5 minutes until the potatoes are just barely cooked.

In the bowl used for the potatoes and onions – don't rinse it – beat the eggs and remaining salt. Fold in the onion-potato mixture and add two-thirds of the peppers and peas; reserve the rest. Heat the remaining oil in the pan used to cook the onion-potato mixture until medium hot. Add the mixture to the pan and shake it every 30 seconds, adding the remaining peppers and peas before the top sets. Cover the pan and cook for a couple of minutes more over medium heat, continuing to shake the pan every 30 seconds.

Preheat oven to 300°.

Remove the pan from the heat and uncover the mixture. Use a rubber spatula to separate the tortilla from the edges of the pan. Spray another 10-inch sauté pan with cooking spray and heat the pan so that it is warm, but not too hot to handle. Place the empty pan upside down over the full sauté pan. Lift the bottom (full) pan by the handle, holding the new warm pan in the center using a towel. Turn the tortilla over in one decisive motion. Before taking off the top pan, lift and tap the two pans gently on the stove to loosen the center of the tortilla. Remove the top pan; if there is any tortilla remaining in it, just use the spatula to fit it back on the larger tortilla.

Turn the stovetop burner on and cook the tortilla for a minute or two. Place the pan in the preheated oven and cook to the desired doneness. Remove the tortilla to a cutting board and let it rest for 10 minutes before cutting it into wedges.

DAWN RANCH LODGE
AGRICULTURE RESTAURANT & BAR

"This was a favorite dish of mine that I enjoyed when I was younger," explains Jason Podsednik of Dawn Ranch Lodge. "My father would prepare it, adding a few twists to this savory favorite. We served it at the café I owned and operated for several years."

16467 River Road (Highway 116)
Guerneville, CA 95446
707-869-0656
dawnranch.com

crispy

PORK BELLY SANDWICH

chef Fernando Plazola

SERVES 4

PORK BELLY

2 ounces canola oil
2 pounds pork belly
2 carrots, diced
1 celery stalk, diced
1 small onion, diced
1 bay leaf
4 thyme sprigs
4 cups chicken stock

GLAZE

2 cups braising liquid
4 ounces crushed piloncillo
   (unrefined Mexican block
   sugar)
1/4 star anise
1 guajillo pepper

SWEET & SOUR PEPPERS

1 ounce canola oil
2 red bell peppers, julienned
1/2 white onion, julienned
1 ounce red wine vinegar
1 ounce sugar

To prepare the pork belly, preheat the oven to 250°.

Heat a large saucepan over medium heat and add the oil. Season the pork with salt and pepper. Sear the pork skin side up until golden brown. Remove the pork from the pan. In the same oil, add the carrots, celery and onion, and sauté them until they're golden brown.

When the vegetables are done, return the pork belly to the pan, seared side up. Add the bay leaf, thyme and chicken stock. Ensure that the stock does not cover the seared side of the pork belly. Place the pan in the oven (uncovered) and cook for 4 hours. Check every hour and add chicken stock if the liquid level drops below 1/2-inch. Remove the pork from the oven and allow it to cool for 15 minutes.

To prepare the glaze, add 2 cups of the liquid from the pork braise to a saucepan. Add the piloncillo and star anise. On an open flame, roast the guajillo pepper until it's brown/black. Remove the seeds and roughly chop the peppers, and add them to the saucepan. Reduce the liquid to 50% over medium heat. Add salt and pepper to taste.

Increase the oven temperature to 400°. With a sharp knife, remove the skin from the pork belly and discard it. Sear the meat, fat side down, until it's golden brown. Brush multiple coats of the glaze on the pork and bake for 20 minutes. Allow to cool.

While the pork is in the oven, prepare the peppers. Heat the oil in a sauté pan on high heat, then add the peppers and onions. Cook for 5 minutes. Add the vinegar and sugar and cook for 3 more minutes. Remove the pan from the heat, and season the pepper mixture with salt and pepper to taste.

To assemble the sandwiches, cut the pork and bread to the desired portions. Spread mayonnaise on the bread, if desired, and add a spoonful of peppers.

ENGLISH TEA GARDEN BED & BREAKFAST

This is a great dish for brunch, as it can be put together the day before, covered and refrigerated up to 24 hours before baking. It's always a delight with our guests, and we serve it almost every Saturday. This is the meatless version, but you can also add 2 cups of cubed ham instead of the mushrooms and onions. Or serve it with bacon, ham or sausage on the side.

119 West Third Street
Cloverdale, CA 95425
800-996-8675
teagardeninn.com

potato, cheddar & mushroom
EGG BAKE

chef Cindy Wolter

vegi

SERVES 8

8 frozen hash brown patties

2 cups sliced mushrooms

3/4 cup green onions, sliced

3 cups shredded Cheddar
  cheese

7 large eggs

1 cup milk

1/2 teaspoon salt

1/2 teaspoon ground mustard

herbs de Provence

Preheat oven to 350°.

Grease a 13-inch by 9-inch baking dish. Place the hash brown patties in the dish in a single layer. Cover the patties with the mushrooms, onions and cheese, in that order.

In a bowl, beat the eggs, milk, salt and mustard. Pour the mixture over the cheese, and sprinkle the top with herbs de Provence. Cover and bake for 1 hour. Uncover the dish and bake for 15 minutes more, or until the edges of the egg are golden brown, and a knife inserted near the center comes out clean. Serve warm.

FARMHOUSE INN & RESTAURANT

At Farmhouse, the kitchen is driven to use seasonal, local and organic produce. We are fortunate to be in Sonoma County, with the bounty of the farms and orchards surrounding us. Nothing is more local than the heirloom pumpkins, squash, apples, honey and berries grown or produced on the Farmhouse owners' ranch just down the road...and the fresh eggs from their chickens are always appreciated by our guests.

7871 River Road
Forestville, CA 95436
707-887-3300
farmhouseinn.com

PUMPKIN WAFFLES
with apple cider sauce

vegi

breakfast chef Laura Danieli

SERVES 4-6

WAFFLES

3 cups flour

1 teaspoon cinnamon

1/2 teaspoon ginger

1/4 teaspoon nutmeg

1 teaspoon salt

1-1/8 teaspoons baking soda

4 teaspoons baking powder

1 cup pumpkin puree

1/2 cup ricotta

6 egg yolks, separated;
   reserve whites

2-1/4 cups milk

3/4 cup vegetable oil

3 tablespoons sugar

APPLE CIDER SAUCE

2 teaspoons cornstarch

3/4 cup local apple cider,
   reduced by half

1/4 teaspoon salt

1 small stick cinnamon

1-1/2 cups dark brown sugar

2 tablespoons corn syrup or
   honey

1 cup cream

1/2 vanilla bean

Whisk the dry ingredients, through baking powder, in medium bowl. Set aside.

In a second bowl, combine the remaining (wet) ingredients, except for the reserved egg whites, and whisk them together until the mixture is smooth. Set aside.

Beat the 6 egg whites until stiff. Combine the pumpkin mixture with the dry ingredients until they're blended, but not over-mixed. Gently fold in the egg whites. Bake in a waffle iron as you do other types of batter.

To prepare the apple cider sauce, combine all the ingredients in a saucepan and heat on the stovetop until the mixture is thick. This can be made ahead so that the flavors can come together. At Farmhouse Inn we serve these waffles garnished with Chantilly cream and candied pecans. During apple season, we get Gravensteins from owner Catherine's orchard and make an apple compote to accompany the dish.

FERN GROVE COTTAGES

Homemade baked goods are always on our breakfast menu, to help our guests start their day in a most satisfying way. This bread offers richness from ripe bananas, sweetness from maple syrup and a tangy kick from cranberries.

16650 River Road (Highway 116)
Guerneville, CA 95446
888-243-2674
ferngrove.com

MAPLE & FRUIT BREAD

vegi

chef Margaret Kennett

MAKES 2 LOAVES;
EACH SERVES 8-10

BREAD
½ cup butter
¾ cup sugar
2 cups all-purpose flour
2 tablespoons maple syrup
3 large eggs
2 ripe bananas, mashed
1 cup dried cranberries

ICING
2 cups powdered sugar
4 tablespoons maple syrup
¼ teaspoon vanilla extract
18 pecan halves, toasted
¼ cup dried cranberries

Preheat oven to 375°.

Coat two 9-inch by 4-inch loaf pans with nonstick cooking spray. Place all the bread ingredients in a bowl and beat well, until the mixture is smooth. Spoon the batter into the prepared pans, and bake for approximately 40 minutes. To test for doneness, insert a wooden skewer into the middle of each loaf; when it comes out clean, the bread is done. Allow the loaves to cool in the pan for 10 minutes.

To prepare the icing, sift the powdered sugar into a bowl. Stir in the maple syrup and vanilla extract, and spoon the topping over the loaves. Decorate with the toasted pecans and dried cranberries and serve.

HAMPTON INN & SUITES

A family tradition for years has been the children making this delicious and simple breakfast for their loved ones on Mother's Day. Enjoy our tradition year-round!

8937 Brooks Road South
Windsor, CA 95492
707-837-9355
windsorcasuites.hamptoninn.com

oatmeal-blueberry
PANCAKES

chef Erin McCauley

vegi

MAKES 4 PANCAKES

4 large egg whites

3/4 cup uncooked oatmeal

1/4 teaspoon salt

1/4 cup blueberries (fresh or
   thawed)

In a medium bowl, beat the egg whites into a stiff foam with a hand mixer. Gently fold in the oatmeal and salt.

Coat a skillet with nonstick cooking spray. Pour the desired amount of batter into the skillet, top with blueberries, and cook each pancake until it's brown; flip and cook the other side. Top each pancake with butter and syrup, and serve with your favorite breakfast meat.

HEALDSBURG COUNTRY GARDENS

Add sparkle to any brunch by dressing up fresh melons with a sauce to complement your entrée. This honey-lime sauce also works beautifully with strawberries, kiwis, bananas and orange segments.

670 Bailhache Avenue
Healdsburg, CA 95448
707-431-8630
hcountrygardens.com

MELON DELIGHT
with honey-lime sauce

vegi

chef Barbara Gruber

SERVES 8

2 large cantaloupe, honeydew and/or other melons

⅓ cup undiluted frozen limeade

⅓ cup honey

⅓ cup salad oil (not olive oil)

1 teaspoon celery seed

Slice the melons or cut them into cubes. Arrange the melon pieces on a serving platter or in individual compote glasses. In a medium bowl, add the remaining ingredients and whisk to a smooth consistency.

To serve, drizzle the sauce on the melons, and pass the extra sauce at the table.

HIGHLANDS RESORT

We are known for our muffins. Seriously. Our email address is Muffins@ HighlandsResort.com. We have baked thousands and thousands of muffins over the years and every year we make up new recipes. Lemon-ginger muffins, apple muffins, pecan sticky muffins, cranberry-almond muffins, pineapple upside-down muffins, pumpkin-white chocolate-almond muffins, orange-pecan muffins, coffee cake muffins and more. Here's one for chocolate lovers.

14000 Woodland Drive
Guerneville, CA 95446
707-869-0333
highlandsresort.com

orange-bittersweet chocolate
MUFFINS

vegi

chef Ken "The Muffin Man" McLean

SERVES 6-12

2 medium-sized oranges, washed

1 cup granulated sugar

1 stick unsalted butter, cold and cut into 8 pieces

2 large eggs

½ cup orange juice

½ cup plain yogurt

2 cups flour

1 teaspoon baking powder

½ teaspoon baking soda

¼ cup bittersweet chocolate, roughly chopped (chocolate chips don't work well)

Preheat oven to 350°.

Zest both oranges. Squeeze the juice from them and reserve.

In a food processor, add the sugar and orange zest and process until the zest is finely chopped. Add the butter and pulse about 10 to 15 times, until the butter is finely chopped. If the butter ends up in a big ball, just break it apart with a hard spatula.

Add the eggs and blend until it all comes together. Add the orange juice and yogurt and blend until combined.

Pour the egg-butter mixture into a large bowl. Sift together and stir in the flour, baking powder and baking soda. Mix until just barely combined. Add the chocolate and mix in. Do not over-mix.

Coat a muffin tin with nonstick cooking spray. Evenly divide the batter in the 12-muffin pan. Bake for 20 to 25 minutes, until the muffin tops are golden and the centers done (a toothpick inserted into the muffin comes out clean). These muffins are best served warm.

HONOR MANSION

For some of our guests, brunch wouldn't be brunch without a glass of sparkling wine – and this zesty egg dish matches beautifully with bubbly. Serve it with tomato wedges and a dollop of sour cream on the side.

891 Grove Street
Healdsburg, CA 95448

707-433-4277
honormansion.com

SANTA FE BAKE
with sun-dried tomato sauce

vegi

chef Cathi Fowler, innkeeper

SERVES 6

EGGS

8 eggs

2 cups heavy cream

1/2 chopped onion

1/2 can diced green chilies
   (large) or 1 small can

1-1/4 cups mixed cheese
   (Cheddar & Monterey Jack;
   save 1/2 cup for topping)

TOMATO SAUCE

1 15-ounce can tomato sauce

2 tablespoons chopped
   sun-dried tomatoes
   (packed in oil)

1 cup half and half

1/2 cup sour cream

2 teaspoons sugar

1 rounded tablespoon
   sun-dried tomato pesto
   (if available)

Preheat oven to 350°.

Spray an 8-inch by 8-inch pan with nonstick cooking spray.

Combine all the egg ingredients in a blender, except for 1/2 cup of the cheese. Pour the mixture into the pan and sprinkle the remaining cheese over the top. Bake the eggs for 1 hour.

While the eggs cook, prepare the sun-dried tomato sauce. Combine all the ingredients in a saucepan, bring to a simmer, and keep the sauce hot until the eggs come out of the oven.

To serve, cut the Santa Fe Bake into 6 squares and place each on a plate. Pour the warm tomato sauce over the top of each square, and pass around the remainder sauce for those who enjoy saucier eggs.

HOPE-MERRILL HOUSE

Baking is a foolproof way to prepare an omelet – no stirring of the eggs in a pan, and no flipping, slipping or sliding. This recipe also allows the cook to make several individual-serving omelets and have them ready at the same time to feed a crowd.

21253 Geyserville Avenue
Geyserville CA 95441
707-857-3356
hope-inns.com

BAKED CHEESE OMELET

vegi

chef Cosette Trautman-Scheiber

SERVES 1

2 eggs
2 tablespoons milk or half
  and half
salt and pepper to taste
⅛ cup shredded Cheddar
  cheese

Preheat oven to 400°.

Spray an individual custard cup with cooking oil. For each omelet, break two eggs into a small bowl. With a fork, beat the milk into the eggs. Add salt and pepper to taste.

Pour the mixture into the custard cup and sprinkle the top with the shredded cheese. Place the custard cup on a baking sheet and place the sheet on the lower shelf of the oven. Bake for 25 minutes, or until the omelet is puffy and lightly browned.

Either serve the omelet in its cup, or remove it from the cup and place it on a plate.

INN AT OCCIDENTAL

We were reading The Big Book of Breakfast and came across this recipe. We took it up a few notches and have been serving it to great guest reviews. A television personality from Texas loved it so much, she featured it on her show and blog.

3657 Church Street
Occidental, CA 95465
707-874-1047
innatoccidental.com

orange cream-filled
FRENCH TOAST
with orange sauce

chef Tina Yee Wolsborn

vegi

SERVES 8-10

FRENCH TOAST

4 ounces cream cheese,
   room temperature
1 tablespoon orange juice
1 tablespoon sugar
2 tablespoons orange
   marmalade
1 teaspoon orange zest
1 large loaf sourdough bread,
   unsliced
4 large eggs
1/2 cup milk
1/2 cup half and half
1 tablespoon sugar
1 teaspoon almond extract
2 tablespoons butter
   (or more as needed)

ORANGE SAUCE

2 cups orange juice
1/2 cup butter, melted
3 tablespoons cornstarch
2/3 cup sugar
1/4 cup maple syrup

To prepare the French toast, combine the cream cheese, orange juice, 1 tablespoon of sugar, marmalade and orange zest, and set aside.

Slice the end from the loaf of bread and discard. Cut the next slice 1/2-inch thick, but not all the way through. Cut the following slice 1/2-inch thick and all the way through — you want to create a pocket for the filling. Slice the rest of the loaf in this alternating manner.

Spread about 1 tablespoon of the filling in each pocket, and press together the two bread slices to close them.

In a wide, shallow bowl, whisk together the eggs, milk, half and half, sugar and almond extract. Dip each bread "sandwich" into the egg mixture, turning to coat.

Preheat a griddle over medium heat. Add 1 tablespoon butter to coat the griddle. When the butter foams, add as many bread slices as will fit and cook them until they're lightly browned. Flip them over and cook the other side. Remove the slices and keep them warm until all are cooked.

To prepare the orange sauce, heat the orange juice in a saucepan. In another pan, melt the butter with the cornstarch and cook on medium heat for 1 minute. Add the juice gradually and stir until the mixture thickens, then add the sugar. Bring the mixture to a boil, then reduce the heat to a simmer, cooking for 5 minutes. Remove the pan from the heat and add 1/4 cup maple syrup.

To serve, pour the sauce over the French toast and top the toast with whipped cream, if desired. Crispy bacon makes a great brunch companion.

OLD CROCKER INN

French toast made like a casserole and refrigerated overnight is popular in B&Bs. Our guests like this traditional recipe because the almonds add a bit of crunch and it's not as sweet. We've been tweaking many of our recipes to make them healthier and less dessert-like. This is one of them.

1126 Old Crocker Inn Road
Cloverdale, CA 95425
707-894-4000
oldcrockerinn.com

nut-crusted

FRENCH TOAST

chefs Marcia and Tony Babb

vegi

SERVES 6

TOPPING
½ cup brown sugar
¾ cup oatmeal
¾ cup whole almonds

FRENCH TOAST
1 loaf ciabatta bread
6 eggs
½ cup milk
¼ cup orange juice
½ teaspoon almond extract
  or ¾ teaspoon vanilla
  extract
½ teaspoon cinnamon

To prepare the topping, place all the ingredients in a food processor and pulse until the almonds are finely chopped. Store in an airtight container until you're ready to use the topping.

To prepare the French toast, cut the bread into 1-inch-thick slices. Combine the eggs, milk, juice, extract and cinnamon and blend thoroughly.

Sprinkle 1/4 cup of topping onto a large plate. Dip each slice of bread into the egg mixture and let the excess drip off. Squeeze gently to make sure the center of the bread is moistened, and then coat both sides with topping. Place the slices on a baking sheet for 10 minutes before cooking.

Cook the bread slices on a griddle on medium heat for about 5 minutes. Turn the slices over and cook until browned on both sides. Turn the heat down if the coating gets too brown before the center is cooked.

Serve the French toast with powdered sugar, fresh berries, peaches or sautéed apples on top, and pork sausages on the side. Make syrup available on the table.

The remaining topping can be used for other recipes.

THE RAFORD INN BED AND BREAKFAST

This muffin is always a hit with our guests, because it is moist, flavorful and full of healthy ingredients.

10630 Wohler Road
Healdsburg, CA 95448
800-887-9503
rafordinn.com

morning glorious
MUFFINS

chef Rita Wells

vegi

MAKES 24 MUFFINS

1-3/4 cups flour
1 cup whole wheat flour
3/4 cup sugar
2-1/2 teaspoons baking soda
1 teaspoon baking powder
2-1/2 teaspoons cinnamon
1/2 teaspoon salt
2-1/3 cups carrots, grated
2-1/3 cup apples, peeled
   and grated
2/3 cup shredded coconut
2/3 cup raisins
2/3 cup raw, unsalted
   sunflower seeds
3 eggs, beaten
1/2 cup canola oil
1 teaspoon vanilla
3/4 cup unsweetened
   applesauce
3/4 cup plain or vanilla yogurt

Preheat oven to 325°

In large bowl, combine the flours, sugar, baking soda, baking powder, cinnamon and salt, and mix well.

In a separate bowl, combine the carrots, apples, coconut, raisins and sunflower seeds. Add the beaten eggs, oil, vanilla, applesauce and yogurt. Add the wet ingredients to the dry, and stir until just moistened.

Divide the batter into 24 greased muffin cups and bake 20 to 25 minutes, or until a toothpick inserted into the middle of a muffin comes out clean.

RIO VILLA BEACH RESORT

I grew up in Oklahoma and it seems that everyone in my extended family liked to cook. Aunt Wanda lived with us for a short while when I was little and she worked at the small bakery in town. On Saturday mornings she would make a big breakfast and we begged her to make her fried dough and let us kids help. We would end up with powdered sugar everywhere as we laughed and ate ourselves silly. We called this messy confection Okie Doughs, and I share this recipe by way of my dear Aunt Wanda.

20292 Highway 116
Monte Rio, CA 95462
877-746-8455
riovilla.com

aunt wanda's
OKIE DOUGHS

chef Ron Moore

vegi

SERVES 8-12

½ cup warm water
1 package yeast
2-½ cups flour
2 teaspoons baking powder
¼ teaspoon baking soda
½ teaspoon salt
½ stick of butter, softened
¼ cup sugar
1 cup milk
1 tablespoon sour cream
2 cups (approximate) canola
   oil for frying
desired toppings: powdered
   sugar, cinnamon sugar,
   frosting, nuts, etc.
assembly line helpers

In a small bowl, dissolve the yeast in the warm water and set it aside.

In a medium bowl, mix together the flour, baking powder, baking soda and salt, and set aside.

Cream the butter and sugar in a mixer on medium speed. Add the milk, sour cream and yeast mixture. Reduce the mixer speed to slow and mix in the dry ingredients just until everything is combined.

On a floured surface, roll the dough to 1/2-inch thickness. Let the dough rest while you pour oil in a medium sauté pan with deep sides and set the heat to medium. Arrange an assembly line starting with a platter covered with paper towels, followed by shallow bowls of powdered sugar, cinnamon sugar, frosting, chopped nuts or whatever sounds good.

Once the oil is shimmering, cut donut shapes in the dough, using a juice or shot glass. In batches of two or four, drop the dough pieces quickly into the hot oil. They cook very quickly, so turn each one over within a matter of seconds, using a long fork. Remove the pieces from the oil onto the paper towels and let your helpers start moving them down the assembly line, dipping the donuts into the toppings and placing them on a serving plate. Fry the remaining odd shapes of dough and decorate similarly.

SANTA NELLA HOUSE BED AND BREAKFAST

When we serve Bob's Enchiladas Huevos, I make this recipe to complement our breakfast. I sprinkle a little paprika over the top to add some color before baking the cornbread, and make honey butter to serve on the side.

12130 Highway 116
Guerneville, CA 95446
707-869-9488
santanellahouse.com

MEXICAN CORNBREAD

baker Betsy Taggart

SERVES 12

1 8-ounce can creamed corn

3/4 cup milk

1/3 cup melted and cooled
   bacon fat

1 cup cornmeal

1/2 cup polenta (course
   ground)

2 eggs, lightly beaten

1 teaspoon baking powder

1 teaspoon salt

1 teaspoon sugar

1/4 teaspoon baking soda

1 cup shredded sharp Cheddar

1/2 cup Parmesan cheese,
   grated

1 4-ounce can diced green
   chilies

1/8 teaspoon paprika

Preheat oven to 375°.

In a large bowl, mix all the ingredients except for the paprika, blending well.

Transfer the batter to a greased 8-inch by 11-inch baking dish, and sprinkle the paprika over the surface of the batter.

Bake the cornbread for 30 minutes, or until a toothpick inserted into the center comes out clean. Serve warm, with honey butter, if desired.

SONOMA ORCHID INN

This is the perfect tart for a chilly morning, with warm potatoes and freshly picked asparagus comforting your soul. For this recipe, we use organic eggs from our own free-range chickens.

12850 River Road
Guerneville, CA 95446
888-877-4466
sonomaorchidinn.com

potato & asparagus
TART

chef Dana Murphy

vegi

SERVES 6

1 pound potatoes, peeled
   and cut into chunks
1 pinch salt
1 pound asparagus spears,
   woody ends removed
8 ounces filo pastry
1/2 cup butter, melted
1/4 cup Gruyere cheese
2/3 cup Cheddar cheese
4 large eggs
8 ounces heavy cream
1 teaspoon nutmeg,
   freshly grated
freshly ground pepper

Put the potatoes into a pan of salted boiling water, covered by at least 4 inches of water, and cook for 11 minutes or until done. Remove them to a colander to drain. Add the asparagus to the pan and cook them for 4 minutes. Drain the asparagus.

Preheat the oven to 375°.

In an ovenproof dish, layer the sheets of filo pastry, brushing them with melted butter as you go and letting about 1 inch of pastry hang over the edge. You want to build the pastry about 5 or 6 layers thick. Cover the baking dish with a damp kitchen towel until you're ready to fill it.

Mash the potatoes with the two cheeses, leaving some lumps, as they add texture to the tart. In a separate bowl, mix together the eggs and cream and stir into the cheesy potatoes. Grate in the nutmeg, season well with pepper, and mix together.

Spread the potatoes over the filo pastry, and bring up the sides of the filo and scrunch them together to form a rim. Place the cooked asparagus spears on top of the filling, making sure to cover it all. Brush the asparagus with the remaining melted butter and bake for 20 minutes, or until the tart is golden and crisp. Allow to rest for 10 minutes, and serve just as you would a quiche.

VILLAGE INN & RESTAURANT

We are blessed to live in Sonoma County, with its abundance of outstanding local produce. This recipe celebrates West County coastal mushroom foraging. To learn more, visit sonomamushrooms.org.

20822 River Boulevard
Monte Rio, CA 95462
707-865-2304
villageinn-ca.com

MUSHROOM BISQUE

chef John Crespo

MAKES 2 QUARTS

4 ounces unsalted butter
2 yellow onions, rough dice
1 bunch celery, rough dice
3 ounces garlic, chopped
3 ounces Sherry wine
1-1/2 pounds mushrooms
  of choice, sliced
1 tablespoon salt to taste
1 tablespoon freshly ground
  black pepper
1/2 ounce fresh parsley,
  chopped
1/2 tablespoon ground thyme
1 tablespoon fresh thyme
  leaves
1/2 tablespoon oregano
1/2 tablespoon dill, chopped
1/2 tablespoon tarragon
8 ounces chicken stock
1 quart heavy cream

In a stock pot, melt the butter over medium heat and add the onions, celery and garlic. Cook the vegetables to soften them, then deglaze the pan with the Sherry.

Add the mushrooms and cook until they're tender. Add the salt, pepper and herbs (parsley, thyme, oregano, dill, tarragon). Stir to combine, and add the chicken stock and cream. Stir again, and simmer the mixture for 20 minutes.

Remove the bisque from the heat and puree it with an immersion blender. Adjust the thickness of the soup with water, if necessary. Adjust the seasoning with salt and pepper to taste, and serve.

VINE HILL INN BED & BREAKFAST

This is a great recipe with which to experiment. Feel free to substitute any vegetables you have on hand.

3949 Vine Hill Road
Sebastopol, CA 95472
707-823-8832
vine-hill.com

SPINACH FRITATTA

vegi

chef Kathy Deichmann

SERVES 8

10 eggs
½ cup flour
1 teaspoon baking
   powder
1 teaspoon onion powder
1 teaspoon garlic powder
¼ cup butter or margarine,
   melted
3 cups cottage cheese
1 cup cooked fresh spinach or
   10 ounces frozen spinach,
   thawed and squeezed dry
1 bunch green onions,
   chopped
½ yellow bell pepper,
   chopped
½ red bell pepper, chopped
12 ounces shredded Swiss or
   Monterey Jack cheese

Preheat oven to 350°.

In a food processor, blender or mixer, combine the eggs, flour, baking powder, onion powder, garlic powder, butter and 1 cup of the cottage cheese; blend well.

Pour the mixture into a large bowl and add the remaining ingredients. Mix well. Divide the mixture into two greased 10-inch pie pans and bake for 40-45 minutes, or until set. Serve with salsa.

VINTNERS INN / JOHN ASH RESTAURANT

At the restaurant, we serve these duck confit hash cakes with a poached farm egg, heirloom beet carpaccio and arugula. We source as many local products as possible for our menus, including Petaluma's Liberty Ducks; they're among the most tender and flavorful in the country. Begin this dish 24 hours in advance.

4330 Barnes Road
Santa Rosa, CA 95403
707-527-7687
vintnersinn.com

liberty duck confit
HASH CAKES
chef Thomas Schmidt

SERVES 4

CONFIT
2 Liberty Duck legs
¼ cup salt
2 tablespoons fresh ground
    black pepper
2 tablespoons dried thyme
rendered duck fat

HASH CAKES
2 to 3 large Yukon Gold potatoes,
    peeled and quartered
salt and pepper to taste

BEET CARPACCIO
2 medium heirloom beets
    (Bull's Blood or Detroit Red)
olive oil
salt and pepper
4 free-range farm eggs
2 to 3 tablespoons white vinegar
1 bunch arugula, washed and
    trimmed
1 bunch chives
fleur de sel (sea salt)

VINAIGRETTE
2 tablespoons walnut oil
6 tablespoons apple cider vinegar
1 tablespoon pomegranate syrup
salt and pepper

To prepare the confit, start one day ahead. Generously season the duck legs with salt, pepper and thyme and place them in a non-reactive dish. Cover the dish with plastic wrap and refrigerate for 24 hours.

The next day, preheat the oven to 350°. Wash off the seasoning from the legs and pat them dry. Place them in a casserole dish fitted with a lid. Melt the duck fat in a saucepan and pour it over the legs. Put the lid on the casserole and place the dish in the preheated oven for 2 hours, or until the duck legs are very tender. Allow them to cool in the fat. (This can be done 1 to 2 weeks in advance; just store the duck legs in the refrigerator, ensuring that they remain covered in fat).

To prepare the hash cakes, remove the duck from the fat and pull the meat off the bones; discard the bones and skin. Shred the meat by hand and set it aside. Retain the fat.

Boil the potatoes in lightly salted water until they're soft. Drain and run them through a food mill. In a bowl, mix equal amounts of duck and potatoes until they're well combined. Add some duck fat to make the mixture pliable, and season it with salt and pepper. Let the mixture cool, and form it into patties approximately 3 inches in diameter and 1-inch thick. Cover and keep them cold.

To prepare the beet carpaccio, preheat the oven to 350°. Clean the beets, leaving 1/2-inch of the stems and tails intact. Place each beet on an individual piece of aluminum foil approximately 9 inches square. Drizzle each beet with olive oil and season with salt and pepper. Wrap the foil tight around the beets and bake for 1-1/2 hours, or until just tender. Let the beets cool slightly, then unwrap and peel them.

Meanwhile, heat a large nonstick pan to medium. Cover the bottom of the pan with duck fat. Place 4 hash cakes in the fat and cook them until they're brown and crispy on both sides. At the same time, bring a large pot of water to a boil, add 2 to 3 tablespoons white vinegar, and turn the heat down to a low simmer.

While the duck cakes cook, blend all the vinaigrette ingredients in a small bowl. Slice the beets thin on a mandolin or with a knife. Overlap them in concentric circles on 4 plates, covering the whole plate. Dress the beets generously with the vinaigrette and place a duck cake in the middle of each plate.

Crack the eggs into 4 small bowls and gently transfer them to the lightly simmering water to poach. Arrange the arugula around the duck cake. Top each cake with a poached egg, snipped chives and fleur de sel. Serve immediately.

WEST SONOMA INN & SPA

This is a weekend brunch favorite of ours when we lived in foggy San Francisco. It's simple and easy to cook, and has great flavor. The prep and cook time is only about 25 minutes. When chopping the chile pepper, be careful not to rub your eyes with your hands, and make sure to wash those hands immediately after working with the chile.

14100 Brookside Lane
Guerneville, CA 95446
707-869-2470
westsonomainn.com

SPICY SCRAMBLED EGGS vegi

chefs Karen O'Brien and Naveed Haneef

SERVES 4

6 large eggs

additional 2 egg whites

¾ teaspoon salt
   (not sea salt)

pinch black pepper

2 tablespoons milk

2 tablespoons butter

2 shallots, finely chopped

2 medium tomatoes,
   chopped

1 whole green serrano chile,
   finely chopped

1 clove garlic, finely chopped

Break the eggs into a medium mixing bowl. Add the salt, pepper and milk and beat together with a whisk for about 2 minutes, until the eggs are frothy and evenly colored. Set aside.

Warm a nonstick frying pan over medium heat and add the butter. Let the butter liquefy and coat the bottom surface of the pan. Add the shallots and cook, stirring gently, until they're soft. Add the tomatoes, chile and garlic. Stir occasionally until the tomatoes have broken down into more of a paste.

Add the whisked eggs to the frying pan, on top of the other ingredients. When the eggs begin to set, start scrambling them to create curds or large lumps with the eggs. Use a spatula to move the eggs around and cook them evenly. Continue cooking the eggs until they're completely set.

Serve the eggs warm with lightly buttered flatbread or plain naan bread. Optionally, sprinkle the eggs with shredded cheese or fresh cilantro.

APPETIZERS

Duck Chilaquiles with Cherry-Guajillo Chile Sauce

Alligator Sausage Cheesecake with Shrimp

Dungeness Crab Salad

Spicy Crab Arancini

Arancini di Riso

Kathleen's Sweet & Spicy Grilled Prawns

Point Reyes Blue Cheese Paté

Zinfandel-Braised Pork with Vella Dry Jack Polenta

Red, Smoked & Blue Filet Mignon

Bruschetta with Mushroom Pesto

Wood Stove Fondue with Tri-Color Potatoes

Costeaux French Bakery Focaccia

Swedish Gravlax with Mustard Sauce

ACORN WINERY / ALEGRIA VINEYARDS

Jeff Mall says: "My wife and I have been fortunate to be the culinary and farm consultants for a small boutique resort, Rancho Pescadero, in Pescadero, Baja California. This dish was inspired by Dora, a cook at the resort, whose chilaquiles are the best I've ever had! This is the perfect example of the importance of wine and food pairing. Each are good on their own, but pair the Zinfandel with the deep flavors and richness of the chilaquiles, and together they just pop."

12040 Old Redwood Highway
Healdsburg, CA 95448
707-433-6440
acornwinery.com

DUCK CHILAQUILES
with cherry-guajillo chile sauce

chef Jeff Mall, Zin Restaurant & Wine Bar

Pair with Acorn Winery Heritage Vines Zinfandel

SERVES 4
SAUCE
4 ounces dried Guajillo chiles, seeds and stems removed

2 tablespoons canola oil

1 small yellow onion, small dice

2 cloves garlic, thinly sliced

6 ounces pitted, frozen dark cherries

2 teaspoons Mexican oregano

1-1/2 teaspoons cumin seeds, toasted and ground

2 teaspoons kosher salt

1/2 cup Acorn Heritage Vines Zinfandel

1 cup chicken stock

CHILAQUILES
2 confit cooked duck legs

2 tablespoons unsalted butter

1 small yellow onion, thinly sliced

1 poblano pepper, roasted, peeled, cut into strips

10 corn tortillas, cut into 1/2-inch-wide strips; fried crisp

2 cups Cherry-Guajillo Chile Sauce

1/2 cup crumbled Cotija cheese

To prepare the sauce, preheat the oven to 350°. Place the Guajillo chiles on a cookie sheet and lightly toast them for 15 minutes. Remove the chiles from the oven and place them in a bowl. Cover the chiles with warm water for 30 minutes to rehydrate them. Drain the chiles and discard the water.

Heat a 2-quart saucepan over medium-high heat. Add the oil and onions and cook until the onions are dark golden brown. Add the garlic, cherries, oregano, cumin and salt. Stir and cook for 2 minutes.

Add the wine, chicken stock and drained Guajillo chiles. Bring the mixture to a boil, reduce to a simmer and cook 30 minutes. Puree the sauce in a blender, strain it through a mesh sieve, and season to taste.

To prepare the chilaquiles, remove the meat from the confit duck legs and shred it by hand. Set the meat aside.

Heat a large sauté pan over medium heat. Add the butter and sauté the onion and roasted poblano pepper strips until the onion is translucent. Add the shredded duck and cook for 2 minutes. Add the cherry–chile sauce and bring the mixture to a simmer.

Add the crisp tortilla strips and toss them until they're completely covered in sauce and duck mixture (toss gently, taking care not to break the chips). Continue to cook until the tortillas have absorbed most of the sauce.

To serve, divide the chilaquiles among 4 plates and sprinkle with the crumbled Cotija cheese.

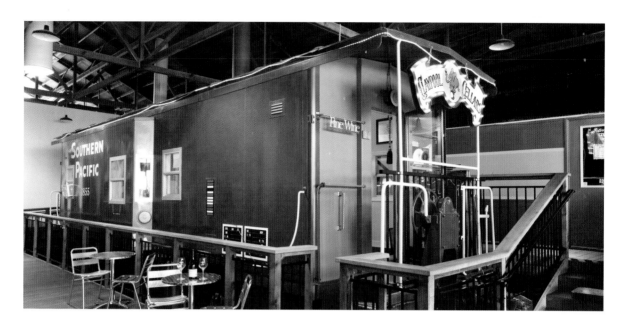

CLAYPOOL CELLARS

Many years ago while in New Orleans for my first Oysterhead performance, we went to dinner at Jacques-Imo's restaurant. The server announced that there were just three slices of Alligator Sausage & Shrimp Cheesecake left. "Who the hell wants that?" we all thought. Yet Jack, the owner, brought out two slices of the cheesecake anyway. I'd had a few glasses of wine, so I popped a chunk into my mouth, and it was quite possibly the most enjoyable bit of food I've ever had. Be brave. Try it yourself.

6761 Sebastopol Avenue, Suite 111
Sebastopol, CA 95472
707-861-9358
claypoolcellars.com

ALLIGATOR SAUSAGE
cheesecake with shrimp

chef Jacques Leonardi, Jacques-Imo's Café

Pair with Claypool Cellars Purple Pachyderm Pinot Noir

SERVES 12

1-1/3 cups bread crumbs

2/3 cup Parmesan cheese, grated

4 ounces butter, melted

1-1/2 pounds cream cheese, softened

3-1/3 eggs

2/3 cup cream

1/3 cup smoked Gouda cheese, grated

1 onion, medium diced

1-2/3 green pepper, medium diced

1 yellow bell pepper, diced

1 red bell pepper, diced

1/2 tablespoon chipotle powder

1/2 tablespoon Fajita Magic seasoning

1/2 pound shrimp, diced

1/2 pound alligator sausage, diced (purchase from exotic meat market)

1/3 can green chiles, diced

pinch salt

Preheat oven to 400°.

In a medium bowl, mix the bread crumbs and Parmesan cheese. Add the butter and press the mixture into a 10-inch springform pan. Bake for 10 minutes to set the crust. Increase the oven temperature to 450°.

In a clean bowl, whisk the cream cheese until it's smooth. Add the eggs and whisk, then add the cream and the Gouda. Set aside.

Sauté all the vegetables, through the red bell pepper, with spices, until the vegetables are soft. Add the shrimp and cook until just done.

Add the sausage and green chiles to the vegetable-shrimp mixture. Fold in the cream cheese mixture and allow it to cool. Wrap foil around the springform pan to prevent leakage and pour the ingredients into the pan.

Bake the cheesecake in a water bath (a 2-inch hotel pan filled 1/3 with water) for 1-1/2 to 2 hours. It's done when a knife inserted in the center comes out clean and the filling is set. Let the cheesecake cool. Remove from the spring mold, cut it into 12 pieces, and serve.

GUSTAFSON FAMILY VINEYARDS

This crab salad really makes our rosé "pop." The crab should be fresh to maximize the wine's bright fruit flavors, and finding fresh Dungeness isn't a problem when you're in our neck of the woods. We made this salad for our first public event and people kept coming back for more. Sure, we'd like to think it's just the rosé, but we know it is really the overall experience of a perfect pairing. Enjoy!

9100 Skaggs Springs Road
Healdsburg CA 95448
707-433-2371
gfvineyard.com

dungeness
CRAB SALAD

chef Dan Gustafson

Pair with Gustafson Family Vineyards Estate Rosé of Syrah

SERVES 4-6

⅓ cup mayonnaise, or as
 needed to bind
1 tablespoon Dijon mustard
½ pound Dungeness
 crabmeat, cleaned and
 cartilage removed
⅓ cup finely diced celery
zest of 1 lemon
1 to 2 tablespoons lemon
 juice
2 tablespoons fresh chives,
 chopped
1 tablespoon flat-leaf parsley,
 chopped
salt and freshly ground black
 pepper to taste
cayenne pepper to taste
12 to 18 Belgian endive leaves

In a large bowl, combine the mayonnaise and mustard, and then add the crabmeat, celery, lemon zest, 1 tablespoon of lemon juice, chives and parsley. Add the remaining lemon juice, salt, black pepper, and cayenne to taste. Cover the bowl with plastic wrap and refrigerate until it's time to serve the salad. It can be prepared up to 1 day ahead of time, but tastes best when served within 6 hours.

Just before serving, spoon the crab salad onto the endive leaves and arrange them on a platter. For a different presentation, spoon the salad onto crispy wonton crackers or slices of toasted bread.

HAWLEY WINERY

Arancini are fried risotto balls, and they are extremely popular in Italy, with various regions creating their own versions. Local Dungeness crab gives our arancini a California twist on an Italian favorite.

36 North Street
Healdsburg, CA 95448
707-473-9500
hawleywine.com

SPICY CRAB ARANCINI

chef Emma Uribe

Pair with Hawley Viognier

MAKES 24 ARANCINI

2 tablespoons olive oil

2 medium yellow onions, small diced

1 box Arborio or Carnaroli rice

½ bottle white wine

4 cups chicken or fish stock

2 pounds Dungeness crab meat

2 tablespoons harissa paste

3 threads of saffron

1 cup grated Parmigiano-Reggiano

juice of 1 lemon

salt to taste

1 bunch Italian parsley, chopped very fine

2 cups all-purpose flour, seasoned with salt and pepper

3 eggs, beaten

2 cups panko bread crumbs

8 cups canola oil

In a large pot over medium heat, add 2 tablespoons of olive oil and the onions. Cook until the onions are translucent. Add the box of rice and stir to coat the grains with oil. Stir in the white wine with a wooden spoon and keep stirring until all of the liquid has evaporated.

Begin adding the stock ladle by ladle, allowing most of the liquid to evaporate before adding another ladle. Stir the risotto constantly to ensure it will become creamy and cook evenly.

Once the rice has become al dente, about 15 to 20 minutes, take it off the heat. Add the crab meat, harissa paste, saffron, Parmigiano, parsley, half of the lemon juice and salt. Stir to incorporate all of the ingredients, transfer the mixture to a bowl and allow it to cool completely in the refrigerator.

Meanwhile, set up a breading station. Fill 1 bowl with seasoned flour, 1 with the beaten eggs and 1 of seasoned bread crumbs. When the risotto has cooled, form it into balls about the size of a golf ball. Dip each one in the flour, then the egg and then the panko. Place the balls carefully on a sheet pan.

In a heavy-bottomed pot, add the canola oil and heat it to 180°. Drop the risotto balls into the oil, 5 or 6 at a time, and fry them until they are golden brown, rotating them slightly every few minutes. Line a large bowl with paper towels and transfer each arancini from the oil to the bowl. While they're still hot, season them with salt and the remaining lemon juice, and serve.

HOP KILN WINERY

These crisp, cheese-filled risotto croquettes are called arancini because they look like little oranges. The Italian word for orange is arancia and arancini means "little orange." These risotto balls are one of chef Renzo's family favorites. To merge the flavors with our Pinot Noir, he adds the wine to the risotto cooking liquid. Crunchy, creamy and cheesy, these arancini are the perfect Italian treat.

6050 Westside Road
Healdsburg, CA 95448
707-433-6491
hopkilnwinery.com

ARANCINI DI RISO
(risotto appetizer)

chef Renzo Veronese

Pair with HKG Estate Russian River Valley Pinot Noir

MAKES 20 ARANCINI

TOMATO SAUCE
1 tablespoon olive oil
1/2 medium white onion, diced
1 clove garlic, minced
1 32-ounce can whole tomatoes
salt and pepper to taste

ARANCINI
1 tablespoon olive oil
1/2 medium white onion, diced
2 cups Arborio rice
6 cups chicken stock
2 cups HKG Pinot Noir
1 bay leaf
salt and pepper to taste
1/2 cup Parmesan cheese, grated
1 cup fresh peas (or frozen if
   fresh not available)
4 ounces mozzarella cheese, cut
   into 1/4-inch cubes
4 slices ham, cut into 1/4-inch cubes
1 quart vegetable or canola oil
   for frying
2 tablespoons flour
2 eggs, beaten
2-1/2 cups panko bread crumbs

To prepare the tomato sauce, heat the oil in a saucepan, add the onion and garlic, and sauté over medium heat until the onions are translucent. Add the tomatoes and season with salt and pepper. Simmer for 45 minutes. Puree the mixture and set it aside.

To prepare the arancini, heat the oil in a large, heavy-bottom saucepan. Add the onions and sauté over medium heat until the onions are soft. Add the rice and stir continuously for 2 minutes, coating the rice. Add 3 cups of the chicken stock and all of the Pinot Noir. Bring the mixture to a boil, and add the bay leaf, salt and pepper. Stir continuously.

When the stock and wine have been absorbed, add the remaining 3 cups of chicken stock, 1 cup at a time, stirring and cooking until the liquid has evaporated before adding more. Add the Parmesan. Transfer the mixture to a baking sheet and let it cool.

Using an ice cream scooper, scoop a ball of risotto into your hand. Make an impression with your thumb in the center and place a couple of peas, ham and mozzarella cubes in the middle of the ball. Enclose the ball and roll it in your hand into the size of a golf ball. Place the ball on a baking sheet. Dip the scooper in cold water, wet the palm of your hand with water, and repeat with the remaining risotto.

Heat the canola oil to 350° in a large, deep saucepan. Place the flour, beaten eggs and panko in separate bowls. Dredge each risotto ball in the flour, then the egg, and roll them in the panko until they're completely coated. Fry the arancini in small batches until they're golden brown, approximately 3 minutes, turning as needed. Using a slotted spoon, transfer the aranini to paper towels to drain. Serve with the tomato sauce.

KELLEY AND YOUNG WINES

I developed this recipe for a TV appearance at KABC in Arizona. The show highlighted our "Garden to Table" philosophy; although we don't raise prawns, we're able to grow everything else in the recipe, including the olive oil, honey, and of course, the wine. I believe it is so important to use wild prawns; their flavor is incomparable to farmed prawns.

428 Hudson Street
Healdsburg, CA 95448
707-433-2364
kelleyyoungwines.com

kathleen's sweet & spicy
GRILLED PRAWNS

chef Kathleen Kelley Young

Pair with Kelley & Young Kathleen Rosé

SERVES 8-10

1 pound fresh wild prawns
  (16-20)
2 to 3 serrano chiles
  (green and/or red)
1 to 2 green onions
  (white & tender green)
3 tablespoons olive oil
juice from 1 Meyer lemon
3 tablespoons honey
2 tablespoons cilantro leaves,
  chopped
salt to taste

Wash the prawns, pat them dry and set them aside.

Clean the chiles by removing the stem end, and using a small knife, remove the white membrane and seeds. Caution: If you are sensitive to chiles, wear latex gloves for this process.

Slice the chilies and chop the onions, and set them aside.

Prepare the marinade by mixing the olive oil, lemon juice, honey and chopped cilantro in a medium non-reactive bowl. Add the prawns, chiles and onions, and toss to coat. Cover the bowl with plastic wrap and let it sit in the refrigerator for up to 24 hours, tossing occasionally to recoat the prawns.

When you're ready to cook the prawns, place them on metal or pre-soaked bamboo grilling skewers. Heat a grill to medium-hot and grill the prawns for 2 to 3 minutes per side. Do not overcook! They will continue cooking once they are removed from the heat.

Remove the prawns from the skewers and serve them with a sweet and spicy dipping sauce or mango salsa.

KORBEL CHAMPAGNE CELLARS

The fruits and nuts in this paté bring out the many characteristics of our sparkling red wine. And who doesn't love blue cheese with their favorite red wine? Serve this on a baguette or crostini. If Point Reyes is not available, use your favorite blue cheese. Prepare the paté one day before you plan to serve it.

13250 River Road
Guerneville, CA 95446
707-824-7000
korbel.com

point reyes
BLUE CHEESE PATÉ

chef Robin Lehnhoff-McCray

vegi

Pair with Korbel Rouge California Champagne

SERVES 8-10

16 ounces Point Reyes Blue
  Cheese, crumbled
8 ounces cream cheese
2 cups Korbel Rouge
½ cup dried cranberries
½ cup dried cherries
½ cup toasted walnuts
½ cup toasted whole
  almonds
½ cup toasted pecans
½ cup golden raisins
½ cup dried apricots,
  chopped
¼ cup toasted pumpkin
  seeds
1 tablespoon fresh rosemary,
  chopped
2 teaspoons cracked black
  pepper

Bring the two cheeses to room temperature in a mixing bowl. In a small saucepan, bring the wine to a boil and add the cranberries and cherries. Remove the pan from the heat and let the mixture rest until it's completely cool. Strain the fruit from the wine — save the wine — and add the fruit to the cheeses. Return the wine to the saucepan and cook it until it is reduced by half. Set the pan aside to cool, then refrigerate.

Add the remaining dried fruit and nuts to the cheeses. Slowly mix the ingredients with a paddle attachment just until the fruit and nuts are incorporated. Add the black pepper and rosemary.

Remove the paté from the mixer bowl and press it into a loaf pan that has been lined with plastic. Chill the paté overnight. When you're ready to serve it, remove the paté from the pan and pour the cooled Rouge reduction over the top. Garnish with more nuts, if desired.

QUIVIRA VINEYARDS & WINERY

The inspiration for this recipe is the marriage of two things we love most — amazing wine and food! Our biodynamic farming methods and motivation to make distinctive wines guide us in everything we do. Visitors enjoying appetizers on the patio or in the garden with a bottle of our Dry Creek Zinfandel is a common sight at Quivira. Prepare the pork a day in advance.

4900 West Dry Creek Road
Healdsburg, CA 95448
707-431-8333
quivirawine.com

ZINFANDEL-BRAISED PORK
with vella dry jack polenta

chef Tim Vallery, Peloton Catering

Pair with Quivira Dry Creek Valley Zinfandel

MAKES 46 PORTIONS

PORK

4 pounds pork butt, tied

kosher salt and fresh ground
   black pepper

extra-virgin olive oil, as needed

2 carrots, medium dice

2 celery stalks, medium dice

1 yellow onion, medium dice

4 garlic cloves, rough chopped

2 tablespoons tomato paste

1 bottle Quivira Dry Creek Valley
   Zinfandel

12 to 24 ounces beef or veal stock,
   as needed

POLENTA

2 tablespoons olive oil

$1/2$ cup shallots, finely chopped

$1/3$ cup garlic, finely chopped

1 tablespoon tomato paste

1 cup Quivira Dry Creek Valley
   Zinfandel

3 cups heavy whipping cream

3 quarts chicken or vegetable stock

kosher salt and fresh ground black
   pepper

3 cups Italian course-ground polenta

$1-1/2$ cups mascarpone cheese

$1-1/2$ cups Vella Dry Jack cheese,
   shredded, plus extra for garnish

$1/2$ cup Italian parsley, chopped, plus
   extra for garnish

$1/3$ cup fresh thyme, chopped

Prepare the pork one day ahead.

Preheat the oven to 325°. Generously season the meat with salt and pepper. To a heavy-duty, 8-quart ovenproof pot, add the olive oil, heat it over medium heat, and sear the pork on all sides.

Remove the meat from the pot and add the carrots, celery, onion and garlic. Sauté the vegetables until the onions are translucent. Add the tomato paste and stir continuously for about 2 minutes. Deglaze the pot with the Zinfandel. Let the mixture reduce by 1/3. Return the meat to the pot and add enough of the stock to cover. Put a lid on the pot and place it in the oven for 2 to 2-1/2 hours. The pork is done when a fork slides in and out effortlessly. Remove the pork from the oven and let it cool in the refrigerator overnight in its cooking liquid.

The next day, preheat the oven to 325°. Remove the meat from the pot and strain the liquid. In an oven-safe pan, add a small amount of the liquid and all of the pork. Cover and place the pan back in the oven. Reduce the remaining liquid to a syrup-like consistency. Chunk the pork into 1- to 2-ounce portions and cover them with the reduced liquid. To prepare the polenta, heat the oil in a heavy-bottom pot. Add the shallots and garlic and sweat them until they're translucent. Add the tomato paste and sauté until the paste takes on a bronze color. Deglaze the pan with the Zinfandel and let the liquid reduce by 1/2. Add the heavy cream and the stock and bring to a boil. Add salt and pepper to taste. Whisk in the polenta and stir constantly until a thick, soupy consistency is achieved, about 30 minutes. Remove the polenta from the heat. Whisk in the mascarpone, Dry Jack and the herbs.

To serve, spoon the polenta on small plates and place a chunk of pork on the polenta. Drizzle the pork with reduced braising liquid and top with the cheese and parsley.

RODNEY STRONG VINEYARDS

Preparation starts one day in advance for this recipe, so that the beef luxuriates in a brine bath overnight, making it buttery-tender and flavorful. You will also need a smoker, yet the extra effort pays off in smoky filet mignon bites that are enhanced by a rich blue cheese spread and tied to our Rockaway Cabernet Sauvignon by a drizzle of Cabernet-cherry preserve.

11455 Old Redwood Highway
Healdsburg, CA 95448
707-431-1533
rodneystrong.com

red, smoked & blue
FILET MIGNON

chef Tim Vallery, Peloton Catering

Pair with Rodney Strong Rockaway Cabernet Sauvignon

MAKES 60 APPETIZERS

FILET MIGNON

3 pounds center-cut filet mignon, trimmed of fat and silver skin

2 cups water

2 cups Rodney Strong Cabernet Sauvignon

3 ounces brown sugar

3 ounces granulated sugar

12 ounces kosher salt

2 bunches fresh thyme

3 bay leaves

2-1/2 pounds ice

CABERNET CHERRY PRESERVE

1 bottle Rodney Strong Cabernet Sauvignon

1 bay leaf

3 sprigs fresh thyme

1/2 cup granulated sugar

2 cups dried cherries, finely chopped

1 teaspoon fresh ground black pepper

BLUE CHEESE SPREAD

5 ounces Point Reyes Blue Cheese

7 ounces cream cheese

4 ounces heavy cream

1 teaspoon kosher salt

1 tablespoon fresh thyme, minced

To prepare the filet mignon, quarter the tenderloin lengthwise to create 4 triangle-shaped pieces. In a large stainless steel pan, heat all the ingredients except the beef and ice to 180°. When all the ingredients are dissolved, remove the pan from the heat and add the ice. Allow the liquid to cool, place the tenderloin pieces in the brine, and refrigerate for 8 to 10 hours.

Remove the filet mignon from the brine and let it air-dry on a rack for at least 1 hour. Generously season the beef with salt and pepper. In a smoker using oak or hickory wood (follow manufacturer's instructions), indirectly smoke the filet until an internal temperature of 135° is reached. Chill the meat for at least 2 hours.

While the beef is chilling, prepare the Cabernet-cherry preserve. In a stainless steel-lined saucepan, bring the wine to a simmer. Add the bay leaf and thyme. Reduce the wine by 1/2, then add the sugar, cherries and black pepper. Let the mixture slowly reduce to a syrup-like consistency. Remove the thyme sprigs and bay leaf, and chill the sauce in the refrigerator.

Approximately 15 minutes before serving the beef, prepare the blue cheese spread. Melt the blue and cream cheeses in a double boiler. In a saucepan, heat the cream to a simmer and add the salt. Combine the cream and cheeses in the double boiler, stir to blend completely, and add the thyme. Let the mixture cool.

To serve, slice a medallion of filet, spread the blue cheese mixture on the meat, and top with a drizzle of Cabernet-cherry preserve.

SBRAGIA FAMILY VINEYARDS

The basic recipe was passed down from my aunt. It was a standard at all our Thanksgiving dinners. There is something about the earthy flavors of the mushrooms with the walnuts that makes this one of my favorite fall recipes. Grilling the mushrooms first imparts a wonderful smoky flavor. You can also use the pesto on grilled beef, or toss it with a little cream and add it to cooked pasta.

9990 Dry Creek Road
Geyserville, CA 95441
707-473-2992
sbragia.com

BRUSCHETTA
with mushroom pesto

chef Tracy Bidia, T & Company

vegi

Pair with Sbragia Home Ranch Chardonnay

SERVES 8-10

8 ounces white button
  mushrooms, quartered
1/4 cup caramelized onions
1/2 cup walnuts, toasted
2 garlic cloves
1-1/2 cups fresh Italian parsley
3/4 cup olive oil
1/2 cup Parmesan cheese,
  freshly grated
salt and freshly ground black
  pepper
36 slices (1/2-inch thick)
  baguette bread

Preheat a grill and lightly coat the mushrooms in olive oil. Grill the mushrooms until they have a smoky aroma and are imprinted with grill marks.

Place the mushrooms, caramelized onions, mushrooms, walnuts, garlic and parsley in a food processor and pulse until the vegetables are coarsely chopped. With the machine running, gradually add 1/2 cup of the oil, blending just until the mushrooms are finely chopped.

Transfer the mushroom mixture to a medium bowl. Stir in the Parmesan. Season the mushroom pesto with salt and pepper to taste. If you're not using the mushroom pesto right away, cover the bowl tightly with plastic wrap to prevent discoloration of the mushrooms.

Preheat a grill pan to medium-high heat. Arrange the bread slices on the pan. Brush the remaining 1/4 cup of oil over the bread slices. Grill them until they're pale golden and crisp, about 5 minutes (you can also do this on an outdoor grill).

To serve, spread the mushroom pesto on the grilled bread slices. Arrange the bruschetta on a platter and garnish with extra Parmesan.

SHELDON WINES

This dish was inspired by the winter of 2005/2006. Russian River Valley roads were flooding from a seemingly endless downpour, so I made a run into town for supplies before the last road to our house was closed. The power went out shortly after, and didn't return for 10 days. Good thing we had a wood-burning stove and plenty of dry wood! I had stocked up heavily on three of our most staple ingredients – cheese, wine and potatoes – and they got us through the storm.

1301 Cleveland Avenue
Santa Rosa, CA 95401
707-865-6755
sheldonwines.com

WOOD STOVE FONDUE
with tri-color potatoes

vegi

chef Dylan Sheldon

Pair with Sheldon Vinolocity Grenache

SERVES 10

POTATOES

1-1/2 pounds mixed miniature
   potatoes (red, gold, purple)
2 tablespoons olive oil
sea salt
black pepper

FONDUE

1 large garlic clove, halved
1 cup dry white wine
1/2 pound Gruyère cheese,
   grated
1/4 pound Emmenthaler
   cheese, grated
1/4 pound Appenzeller
   cheese, grated
1-1/2 tablespoons cornstarch
1 to 2 tablespoons kirsch
   cherry brandy (optional)
1/4 teaspoon nutmeg,
   freshly grated

To prepare the potatoes, preheat the oven or wood stove to 350°.

Give the potatoes a quick scrub under running water and dry them off with paper or kitchen towels. Toss the potatoes with the olive oil, salt and pepper. Transfer them to a baking tray and roast them in the oven for 30 to 40 minutes. Give the tray a shake midway through the roasting period to prevent the potatoes from sticking.

Meanwhile, prepare the fondue. Rub the cut side of the garlic cloves on the inside of a large Dutch oven or heavy-bottom saucepan. Add the wine and bring the liquid to a simmer over medium-high heat.

In a large bowl, toss the grated cheeses with the cornstarch. Add a handful of the mixture at a time to the simmering wine, stirring until the first handful of cheese melts before adding the next. Reduce the heat to medium and stir constantly until the cheeses are completely melted. Add the nutmeg and kirsch, if using, and heat until the fondue is bubbling, about 1 to 2 minutes. Dip the cooked mini potatoes into the fondue, and savor.

TRENTADUE WINERY

In ancient Rome, *panis focaciu* was a flatbread baked in the ashes of the fireplace. In American-English, it is sometimes referred to as *focaccia* bread. Focaccia is widely associated with Italy's Liguria region, although in the provinces of Bari, from which the Trentadue family originated, *focaccia Barese* has several variations, including with tomatoes and olives, and with salt grains and rosemary. Bell pepper, onion and eggplant versions are also popular. Add your favorite ingredients to this basic recipe.

19170 Geyserville Avenue
Geyserville, CA 95441
707-433-3104
trentadue.com

costeaux french bakery
FOCACCIA

vegi

Pair with Trentadue Alexander Valley Sangiovese

SERVES 8-10

2 cups bread flour

¼ teaspoon salt

2 teaspoons olive oil plus
   more for brushing

¾ cup milk

1-¼-ounce package fresh
   active yeast, crumbled

Combine all the ingredients in a large bowl. By hand or with a mixer fitted with a dough hook, mix for 8 to 12 minutes. Finish by hand, kneading the dough until it's smooth.

Put the dough back in the bowl, cover it with plastic wrap or a clean cloth, and place it in a warm spot (preferably 75° or higher). Let the dough double in size. Remove it from the bowl and divide the dough in half. Place each piece on a sheet pan or pizza stone. Flatten and dimple each piece with your hands and fingers to yield two approximately 10-inch rounds.

Preheat the oven to 400°.

Brush the rounds with olive oil and top them with a salt of your choice. Add rosemary, lavender or other herbs, and toppings such as sun-dried tomatoes, goat cheese and olives, or caramelized onions, blue cheese and walnuts. Bake the breads for 30 to 40 minutes, until they achieve the desired level of doneness, then slice and serve.

Focaccia also makes for wonderful sandwich bread. Try it with salmon, bacon, tomato and baby greens.

WEST WINES

In Sweden, it is an old tradition to serve gravlax – pickled salmon — for spring and summer holidays at the "smorgasbord." Today, gravlax is served as an appetizer any time of the year. Like most Swedes, we make it ourselves, as it is simple to do and tastes best that way. Ask your fishmonger to remove the bones from the salmon, which will save you the time of doing it yourself. Allow 48 hours for the fish to cure in the refrigerator.

1000 Dry Creek Road
Healdsburg, CA 95448
707-433-2066
westwines.com

SWEDISH GRAVLAX
with mustard sauce

chef Katarina Bonde

Pair with West Wines Dry Creek Valley Viognier

SERVES 10

GRAVLAX
2 pounds fresh whole salmon
    fillet with the skin, deboned
2 tablespoons sugar
4 tablespoons salt
1 teaspoon white
    peppercorns, crushed
1 bunch dill, chopped

MUSTARD SAUCE
1 tablespoon honey mustard
1 tablespoon white vinegar
salt and ground white pepper
3 tablespoons canola or
    grape seed oil
1 teaspoon Dijon mustard
1 bunch dill, chopped

To prepare the gravlax, wipe the salmon clean with paper towels. With pliers, remove all the surface fat and any remaining bones. Cut the salmon into 2 pieces and place them against each other, flesh to flesh, with the skin side out. Spread the salt, sugar and pepper on one of the fillets and then the chopped dill, then place the other fillet on top. Put the stacked fillets in a large plastic bag and place in the refrigerator for 48 hours, turning over the salmon every 12 hours or so.

Just before you are ready to serve the gravlax, prepare the mustard sauce. In a mixing bowl, add the mustard and vinegar, and season to taste with salt and pepper. Drizzle in the oil under constant mixing with a fork. When the sauce is the consistency of mayonnaise, mix in the dill. Adjust the seasoning with salt or pepper, if necessary.

Remove the salmon from the refrigerator and scrape off the herbs. Cut the fish into thin, slanted slices or 1/2-inch-thick straight cuts, and remove the salmon skin.

Serve the gravlax slices on lightly buttered toast, dark pumpernickel or crackers.

Drizzle a little of the mustard sauce over the top and garnish with a slice of lemon and a sprig of dill.

SOUPS

Pumpkin Red Curry

Harvest Ribollita

Honey Harvest Tomato Bisque

Soupe au Pistou

Chris Hanna's Autumn Corn Chowder

PAG Soup

Roasted Apple & Butternut Squash Bisque

Zin-Marinated Pork & Apple Chili

Chanterelle Soup with Turkey & Cranberry Garnish

Posole

Mushroom & Brie Soup with Truffle Oil

Mushroom-Leek Zuppa

BELLA VINEYARDS & WINE CAVES

Although not always thought of as soups, curries such as this one are wonderful when they're served as one would soup, spooned piping-hot into warm bowls during the chilly days and nights of late fall and winter. This recipe features pumpkin; fairytale and red kuri are the best varieties.

9711 West Dry Creek Road
Healdsburg, CA 95448
707-473-9171
bellawinery.com

PUMPKIN RED CURRY

chef Bruce Frieseke

Pair with Bella Maple Vineyards Zinfandel

SERVES 6

½ cup lime juice
¼ cup sugar
¼ cup fish sauce
2 tablespoons canola oil
2 tablespoons red curry paste
1 tablespoons garlic,
   finely chopped
2 tablespoons lemongrass,
   finely chopped
¼ cup fresh ginger, finely
   chopped
2 cups yellow onion,
   ¼-inch dice
2 kaffir lime leaves
4 cans coconut milk
4 cups pumpkin, ½-inch dice
fresh coriander, julienned
fresh chiles, green onion
   for garnish

In a mixing bowl, blend the lime juice, sugar and fish sauce until the sugar is completely dissolved. Set aside.

In a large, thick, non-reactive saucepot over medium heat, briefly fry the red curry paste in the oil until the paste is slightly toasted and very fragrant. Add the garlic, lemongrass and ginger, and sauté, stirring constantly, for 1 minute. Add the onion and sauté everything together until the onions are translucent.

Add the kaffir lime leaves and coconut milk. Turn up the heat to bring the coconut milk to a simmer. Add the pumpkin and return to a simmer. Allow the mixture to cook for about 4 or 5 minutes, until the pumpkin is just tender. Remove the pot from the heat and stir in the lime juice mixture. Seasoning can be adjusted by adding more tart lime juice, sweet sugar or salty fish sauce.

To serve, ladle the curry into warm bowls and garnish with the chiles, coriander and green onion.

DAVIS FAMILY & ZAZU FARM

In Tuscany, this soup is intended to be a use for all the November bounty of the farm or garden and the newly pressed olive oil. We love it so much that when we moved to Sonoma, John's first goal was to grow everything for this soup himself, including the olives. It is a perfect showcase for our Davis Family/Zazu organic farm here at the winery on the banks of the Russian River... as well as the organic olive oil Guy Davis makes. The dish we serve at the event will all be from the Estate farms - come and savor the true spirit of farm to table with us!

52 Front Street
Healdsburg CA 95448
707-433-3858
daviswines.com

HARVEST RIBOLLITA

vegi

chefs Duskie Estes & John Stewart, Zazu

Pair with Davis Family Vineyards Russian River Valley Pinot Noir

SERVES 4

2 cups fresh shell beans
  (or dry white beans)
2 bay leaves
4 cloves peeled garlic,
  divided
2 stalks celery
2 carrots, peeled
1 onion, peeled
1 leek, white part only
good quality extra-virgin olive
  oil (like Davis Family)
½ Savoy cabbage, cut into
  thin ribbons (chiffonade)
1 bunch lacinato kale,
  stemmed and cut into
  chiffonade
6 cups water
kosher salt and freshly
  ground black pepper
½ loaf day-old rustic bread,
  crust removed

If the beans are dried, cover them with water and soak overnight. Cook the beans with the bay leaves and 2 of the garlic cloves until soft, about 1 hour.

Strain the beans, reserving 1 cup of the liquid to add to the soup.

Process the remaining 2 garlic cloves with the celery, carrot, onion and leek until very fine, but not wet (still with tiny pieces of the vegetables, not a puree). Sauté the vegetables in about 1/4 cup extra-virgin olive oil on medium-low heat until they're fragrant and slightly browned, about 10 minutes. Add the beans and their cooking water, cabbage, kale and water. Simmer for approximately 1 hour. Season to taste with salt and pepper.

Crumble the dried bread into chunks and place a handful of the bread in each bowl.

Ladle the soup over the bread and let it stand for a few minutes while the bread softens and the broth has been absorbed.

Finish each bowl with more olive oil and freshly ground black pepper.

DUTCHER CROSSING WINERY

A hearty harvest soup stirs up fond memories of home for our native Midwest proprietor, Debra Mathy. In celebration of her fifth anniversary at the helm of Dutcher Crossing Winery, her friends at Preferred Sonoma Catering created this warming soup.

8533 Dry Creek Road
Healdsburg, CA 95448
707-431-2700
dutchercreek.com

vegi

honey harvest
TOMATO BISQUE

chef Amber Balshaw, Preferred Sonoma Caterers

Pair with Dutcher Crossing Proprietor's Reserve Cabernet Sauvignon

SERVES 8

½ cup olive oil
½ cup onions, chopped
1-½ teaspoons dill weed
5 cups tomatoes, chopped
4 teaspoons honey
1-¼ cups heavy cream
salt and pepper

In a large pot, sauté the onions and dill weed in the olive oil for 5 minutes, or until the onions are translucent. Add the tomatoes. Reduce the heat and simmer for 15 minutes.

Add the honey and cream, and remove the pot from the heat. Using an immersion blender, puree the bisque to a smooth consistency. Add salt and pepper to taste, and serve hot.

FORCHINI VINEYARDS & WINERY

We usually serve a good-sized bowl of an autumn soup for this event, as soup is a Forchini family favorite. On a stormy November day in Provence, France, we had a comforting lunch that began with a simple, delicious vegetable soup; here is Anita Forchini's modified version of that Provencal soup. If you're pressed for time, you can chop the vegetables in a food processor and substitute prepared pesto for homemade.

5141 Dry Creek Road
Healdsburg, CA 95448
707-431-8886
forchini.com

SOUPE AU PISTOU
(provencal vegetable soup with pesto)

chef Randi Kauppi, Oui Cater

Pair with Forchini Proprietor's Reserve Russian River Valley Pinot Noir

SERVES 8

PESTO
4 cups fresh basil
1 cup Parmesan, grated
1/4 cup extra-virgin olive oil
1 teaspoon kosher salt
2 cloves garlic, chopped
1 plum tomato, cored

SOUP
1/4 cup extra-virgin olive oil
5 cloves garlic, finely chopped
3 medium carrots, peeled and
   finely chopped
2 ribs celery, finely chopped
1 yellow onion, finely chopped
1/2 medium zucchini, chopped
1/4 head Savoy cabbage, thinly
   shredded
8 cups chicken stock
7 whole, peeled canned tomatoes,
   chopped
1 teaspoon kosher salt
1 teaspoon black pepper
1 teaspoon rosemary
1 teaspoon marjoram
1 teaspoon sugar
few drops of chipotle pepper sauce
   (optional)
1/3 cup dried spaghetti, broken
   into pieces
1 15-ounce can cannellini beans

To prepare the pesto, blend the basil, Parmesan, oil, salt, garlic and tomato in a food processor until they are finely ground. Season the pesto with salt and pepper and set aside.

To prepare the soup, heat the oil in a 6-quart saucepan over medium-high heat. Add the garlic, carrots, celery and onions, cover the pan and reduce the heat to medium. Cook the vegetables, stirring occasionally, until they're crisp-tender, 10 to 12 minutes.

Add the zucchini and cabbage and cook, covered, until the cabbage has wilted, 3 to 5 minutes. Add the stock, tomatoes, salt, pepper, rosemary, marjoram, sugar and chipotle sauce (if using) and bring the mixture to a boil. Add the spaghetti and continue to cook for a about 9 minutes, until the pasta is al dente.

Mash half of the beans with a fork and add them to the soup, along with the whole beans. Cook until the soup is warmed through. Adjust the seasonings if necessary.

Ladle the soup into bowls and serve with a dollop of pesto on top.

HANNA WINERY

I am a seasonal eater, cook and wine drinker. During the summer months, Hanna Sauvignon Blanc is our house white, with its tangy flavors and zingy acidity. Come fall, once the weather cools, I crave a lush white, like our Russian River Valley Chardonnay. This corn chowder uses last-of-the-season corn, sweet and hot peppers, and butternut squash to celebrate the fall harvest. The addition of smoky applewood bacon makes this chowder hearty enough to pair with our Pinot Noir.

9280 Highway 128
Healdsburg, CA 95448
707-431-4310

5353 Occidental Road
Santa Rosa, CA 95401
707-575-3371
hannawinery.com

chris hanna's autumn

CORN CHOWDER

chef Chris Hanna

Pair with Hanna Russian River Valley Chardonnay

SERVES 8

6 ears white corn
½ cup diced applewood-
   smoked bacon
1 large onion, diced
1 celery rib, diced
1 cup butternut squash, diced
1 red bell pepper, diced
1 jalapeno pepper, diced
2 small red potatoes, diced
1 cup best-quality chicken
   stock
1 cup heavy cream
1 tablespoon sage, chopped
salt and pepper

Remove the kernels from the corn and set them aside. Break the corn cobs in half and place them in a large saucepan or stockpot with 6 cups of water. Bring to a boil, then reduce to a simmer, and cook for 30 minutes to make a corn stock. Strain the stock and discard the cobs. You should have 5 cups of corn stock.

Sauté the bacon in a large saucepan over medium heat until it's crisp, about 10 minutes. Transfer the bacon to a plate and set it aside. Pour off all but 1 tablespoon of the bacon fat from the pan. Add the onion and cook until it's translucent, about 5 minutes. Add the celery, butternut squash, red pepper and jalapeno pepper and sauté for another 5 minutes.

Add the potatoes, corn kernels, reserved corn stock and chicken stock, and bring to a simmer, cooking until the potatoes are tender, about 10 minutes. Add the reserved bacon, heavy cream and sage, and season with salt and pepper to taste. Serve hot.

HART'S DESIRE WINE

Hart's Desire is full of dreamers, true believers and oddballs. We have found that those who follow their own path seem to gravitate to our door. We always provide a vegan, gluten-free dish so that all Wine Road participants can enjoy it. This soup was invented after a batch of volunteer pumpkins and winter squash emerged from our compost, leaving us with an unexpected bounty.

53 Front Street
Healdsburg, CA 95448
707-433-3097
hartsdesirewines.com

PAG SOUP
(pumpkin apple ginger)

vegi

chef Evan Euphrat, Knife for Hire

Pair with Hart's Desire Alexander Valley Viognier

SERVES 6-8

3 Granny Smith or other
   tart apples
1 onion
1/3 cup water
1 tablespoon garlic, chopped
15 ounces fresh pumpkin
   puree (heirloom preferred,
   but canned OK)
3 cups vegetable stock
1/2 tablespoon fresh grated
   ginger
1 can chickpeas (garbanzo
   beans)
1-1/2 cups mixed seasonal
   vegetables, 1/2-inch dice
salt and pepper
freshly grated nutmeg
ground cinnamon

Peel and dice the apples and the onion. Add them to a large stockpot with the garlic and 1/3 cup of water, and cook until the apples are knife-tender.

Puree the mixture in a food processor and return it to the pot. Add the pumpkin puree, then the vegetable stock and ginger, bring the mixture to a simmer, and add the chickpeas and diced vegetables.

Heat through, and season the soup with the salt, pepper, nutmeg and cinnamon to taste.

HARVEST MOON ESTATE & WINERY

As the seasons change from fall to winter, nothing is more comforting than a bowl of soup and a glass of Zinfandel. This recipe fills that need we all crave. To make this dish vegetarian, substitute vegetable stock for the chicken stock.

2192 Olivet Road
Santa Rosa, CA 95401
707-573-8711
harvestmoonwinery.com

roasted apple & butternut squash
BISQUE

chef Tim Valley, Peloton Catering

vegi

Pair with Harvest Moon Russian River Valley Zinfandel

SERVES 6

2 pounds Granny Smith apples, peeled, cored, halved

5 pounds butternut squash, halved, seeds removed

3 tablespoons olive oil

salt and pepper

1-1/2 pounds yellow onion, diced

1 pound carrots, peeled, diced

1 pound celery, diced

1 gallon chicken or vegetable stock

1/2 gallon apple cider

1 quart heavy cream

cinnamon, ground

nutmeg, freshly grated

Preheat oven to 350°.

Rub the halved apples and squash with 1 tablespoon of olive oil and sprinkle them with salt and pepper. Place them cut side down on a sheet tray and roast in the oven until they're soft.

Meanwhile, in a large stockpot, heat the remaining 2 tablespoons of oil, add the onions, carrots and celery, and cook them until they're translucent, about 5 minutes.

Remove the flesh from the squash and add it, and the apples, to the vegetables. Add the stock and simmer until the liquid is reduced by 1/3. Add the heavy cream and allow the mixture to reduce again by 1/3. Then add the apple cider. Puree the mixture until it's completely smooth, then pass it through a fine-mesh strainer. Add the cinnamon, nutmeg, salt and pepper to taste.

Serve hot with crème fraiche or crisp apple slices on top.

J. KEVERSON WINERY

The credit for this recipe goes to my dear friend, Claudine. She has served this chili to large crowds and everyone just loves it. Originally a dry-rub recipe, we began marinating the pork in our Zinfandel and changing a few ingredients so the heat in it pairs nicely with a spicy Zin. Now this is one of our go-to comfort dishes for casual meals with family and friends. We have received many requests for this recipe, so now it is time to share it.

53 Front Street
Healdsburg CA 95448
707-484-3097
jkeverson.com

zin-marinated
PORK & APPLE CHILI

chef Diane Bard

Pair with J. Keverson Starkey's Court Russian River Valley Zinfandel

SERVES 10-12

2 pounds pork loin, cut into
   ½-inch chunks
2 cups of Starkey's Court 2009
   Zinfandel
1 tablespoon Cajun seasoning
3 tablespoons safflower oil
2 red onions, peeled and
   coarsely chopped
2 large garlic cloves, peeled and
   minced
2 red bell peppers, stemmed,
   seeded and coarsely chopped
1 jalapeno, finely minced
2 large cans (35 ounces each)
   diced fire-roasted tomatoes
3 cups beef stock
4 Granny Smith apples, peeled,
   cored and coarsely chopped
4 bay leaves
2 teaspoons chili powder
2 tablespoons light brown sugar
3 cups cooked or canned kidney
   beans, drained and rinsed
kosher salt

Marinate the pork pieces in Zinfandel overnight in the refrigerator.

Remove the pork from the marinade and place the chunks in a large bowl. Add the Cajun seasoning to the bowl and toss with the meat.

Heat the oil in a large heavy-bottomed stockpot over high heat. Working in small batches, add the pork to the pot and brown the pieces on all sides, about 3 minutes for each batch. Transfer the browned meat along with any juices to a small bowl and set aside.

Add the onion, garlic, bell pepper and jalapeno to the pot and sauté them over medium to medium-high heat until the mixture is fragrant and tender, about 5 to 10 minutes. Stir in the tomatoes and stock, and bring the ingredients to a boil, scraping up any browned bits on the bottom of the pot. Gently simmer for 5 minutes.

Add the apples, bay leaves, chili powder and brown sugar, and continue to simmer until the apples are tender, about 30 minutes. Stir in the beans, the reserved browned meat and accumulated juices, and continue to simmer until the meat is hot and cooked through, 10 to 15 minutes. Season with salt to taste, and serve hot.

LA CREMA TASTING ROOM

Chanterelles are one of my favorite mushrooms. In November, after a couple of good rains, they can be found throughout Sonoma County. This simple soup is great for a cool fall evening, and leftover shredded turkey legs make a delicious garnish. The earthiness of the chanterelles and the cranberries in the garnish complement the red-fruit flavors of the Los Carneros Pinot Noir.

235 Healdsburg Avenue
Healdsburg, CA 95448
707-431-9400
lacrema.com

CHANTERELLE SOUP
with turkey & cranberry garnish

chef Justin Wangler

Pair with La Crema Los Carneros Pinot Noir

SERVES 8

GARNISH

¼ cup red wine, such as Pinot Noir
1 ounce dried cranberries
1 teaspoon butter
1 small shallot, minced
2 ounces fresh chanterelle
   mushrooms
2 ounces fresh cranberries
2 ounces cooked turkey, shredded
2 sprigs thyme, leaves picked
kosher salt

SOUP

¼ cup plus 2 teaspoons canola or
   vegetable oil
2 pounds chanterelle mushrooms,
   cleaned and pulled apart into
   small pieces
3 ounces shallots, peeled and sliced
   thinly
2 medium-sized garlic cloves, peeled
   and sliced thinly
10 stems fresh thyme, leaves picked
   and stems discarded
1 bay leaf
2 tablespoons whole butter
2 teaspoons kosher salt
2 fluid ounces Madeira
½ cup cream
2-½ cups water
¼ teaspoon Sherry vinegar

To prepare the turkey/cranberry garnish, in a small saucepan, bring the red wine to a boil. In a separate bowl, pour the hot wine over the dried cranberries. Set aside to steep at room temperature.

Meanwhile, heat a small sauté pan over medium-high heat. Once the pan is hot, add the butter and heat until the butter browns. Add the shallots and sauté for 1 minute. Once the shallots start to brown, add the fresh chanterelles and sauté for 2 minutes. Add the fresh cranberries and cook for an additional 2 minutes. The cranberries are ready when they start to burst open. Add the shredded turkey and thyme leaves and sauté for 1 minute more. Add the dried cranberries and wine. Once the mixture is hot, season with salt to taste.

To prepare the soup, place a large skillet over medium-high heat. Add 1/4 cup canola oil and heat for 30 seconds. Add the chanterelles and sauté them, tossing occasionally, for 5 minutes, until the mushrooms are lightly browned and fragrant. Remove the skillet from the heat and set aside. In a large saucepot over medium-high heat, add 2 teaspoons of canola oil. Allow to heat for 30 seconds, add the shallots and garlic, and cook until the vegetables are translucent. Add the thyme, bay leaf and butter. Season with salt and stir to combine, cooking for 2 minutes.

Carefully add the Madeira and reduce the wine for 30 seconds. Add the cream, water and chanterelles and bring to a simmer. Simmer for 20 minutes, or until the mushrooms are tender. Remove the bay leaf and carefully transfer the hot soup to a blender. Puree the soup until it's smooth, and adjust the seasoning as desired. Serve the soup hot, garnished with the cranberry and shredded turkey.

MURPHY-GOODE WINERY

This traditional Mexican soup is delicious and pairs wonderfully with the Snake Eyes Zinfandel, as the mild spiciness in the soup is complemented by the fruit in the wine. This is always a fun dish to serve for a large crowd. For smaller groups, feel free to cut this recipe in half.

20 Matheson Street
Healdsburg, CA 95448
800-499-7649
murphygoodewinery.com

POSOLE

Jackson Family Wines Culinary Team

Pair with Murphy-Goode Snake Eyes Zinfandel

SERVES 8

POSOLE

4 cloves garlic, crushed

12 cups chicken broth

½ large white onion, diced

8 ounces dried Guajillo chiles,
   seeds and stems removed

3 pounds pork butt, large dice

16 ounces water

1 tablespoon dried oregano

3 teaspoons kosher salt

2 (16-ounce) cans white hominy

GARNISHES

1 avocado, diced

1 cup cabbage, thinly sliced

1 cup white onion, chopped

8 radishes, sliced

2 limes, cut into wedges

2 tablespoons dried oregano

1 teaspoon dried hot red
   pepper flakes

tortilla chips

In a large pot, combine the garlic cloves, chicken broth, onion and chilies. Simmer 20 minutes. Carefully blend the liquid into a purée. Place the liquid back in a large pot and add the pork butt pieces, water, oregano and salt. Gently simmer, uncovered, until the pork is tender, approximately 2-1/2 hours.

Using tongs, transfer the pork to a cutting board and reserve the broth mixture. Shred the pork. Rinse and drain the hominy. Return the pork to the broth and add the hominy. Season with salt to taste and serve with any or all of the garnishes.

PARADISE RIDGE WINERY

We needed a recipe for the event and after a lengthy delay, time was up. On the last day I came up with this spin on a mushroom soup that I used to prepare at my café in Sebastopol, using Brie cheese to thicken the soup, herbs to showcase the wine notes, Ode to Joy for depth and mushrooms for earthiness. I managed to create a recipe that can make Zinfandel sing; what I didn't expect is how well it pairs with Chardonnay and Pinot Noir, too.

4545 Thomas Lake Harris Drive
Santa Rosa, CA 95403
707-528-9463
prwinery.com

MUSHROOM & BRIE SOUP
with truffle oil

created by Annette McDonnell

Pair with Paradise Ridge Estate Hoenslaars Vineyard Zinfandel

SERVES 8-10

2 whole garlic bulbs
1 bunch green onions, chopped
  (reserve 3 tablespoons)
6 tablespoons shallots
2 cloves garlic, chopped
2 tablespoons butter
2 tablespoons olive oil
1-1/2 cups portobello and
  crimini mushrooms, sliced
1 cup plus 6 tablespoons dry
  Sherry
6 cups chicken broth
1/2 teaspoon cayenne pepper
1/3 teaspoon nutmeg
1/2 teaspoon salt
1/2 teaspoon pepper
2 tablespoons fresh thyme
1 cup whole cream
8 ounces Brie cheese, rind
  removed
2 cups exotic mushrooms
3/4 cup Paradise Ridge Ode
  to Joy or other late-harvest
  Sauvignon Blanc
1 tablespoon white truffle oil

Preheat oven to 350°.

Cut the tops off the garlic bulbs and wrap the bulbs in foil. Bake for 30 to 45 minutes, until the garlic is soft. Remove the skin from the cloves.

In an 8- to 10-quart stock pan over medium heat, sauté the green onions, 4 tablespoons of the shallots and the garlic cloves in 1 tablespoon of butter, 1 tablespoon of olive oil and a dash of salt, until lightly browned. Add the portobello and crimini mushrooms and sauté until the mushrooms are golden brown.

Add 1 cup of the Sherry and simmer the mixture until the Sherry is reduced by half. Add the chicken broth and the cayenne, nutmeg, salt, pepper and thyme. Simmer for 1 hour. Add the cream and Brie and continue to simmer the soup, whisking until the cheese melts and is smooth. Puree the soup with an immersion or standing blender.

In a sauté pan, add the remaining 1 tablespoon of butter, 1 tablespoon of olive oil, 2 tablespoons of green onions and the remaining 2 tablespoons of shallots, and cook until the onions are browned. Add the exotic mushrooms and brown. Deglaze the pan with 3/4 cup Ode to Joy, reduce the liquid by half, and add it to the soup. Add the white truffle oil and stir to blend the ingredients.

To serve, garnish the soup with chopped green onions, a dash of nutmeg and a dash of cayenne.

TOAD HOLLOW VINEYARDS

This super soup was created by our tasting room manager, Jim Costa, and his fiancée, Wendy Beseda. The preparation was inspired by each of their grandmothers, Wendy's "Mama Teddie" and Jim's "Nana." What a wonderful tribute to these two lovely ladies! Their love and traditions live on in this delightful and savory recipe.

409-A Healdsburg Avenue
Healdsburg, CA 95448
707-431-8667
toadhollow.com

MUSHROOM-LEEK ZUPPA
da costa/beseda

vegi

chef Jim Costa

Pair with Toad Hollow Vineyards Francine's Selection Unoaked Chardonnay

SERVES 6

8 ounces shiitake mushrooms

8 ounces portabello mushrooms

8 ounces crimini mushrooms

olive oil to sauté ingredients

½ stick butter or more

3 garlic cloves, minced

2 or 3 leeks, washed and sliced

2 teaspoons fresh thyme, finely chopped

¼ cup flour

4-½ cups vegetable stock, low sodium preferred

1 cup Toad Hollow Chardonnay

1-½ teaspoons kosher or sea salt

freshly ground black pepper

1 cup heavy cream

1 cup half and half

½ cup chopped Italian parsley plus more for garnish

truffle oil to taste

Clean the mushrooms; if they need to be washed, be sure to dry them thoroughly! Separate the stems, trim off the bad parts, and chop the stems. Slice the mushrooms in 1/4-inch-thick pieces. Cut the larger ones into bite-size pieces. Set the mushrooms aside.

In a large pot, heat some olive oil and butter and sauté the garlic. Add the sliced leeks, both the white and green parts. Sauté the leeks over low heat for about 10 minutes, until they start to turn slightly brown.

In a separate pan, cook the sliced mushrooms and thyme until the mushrooms are brown. Add a dash or two of wine and deglaze the pan for about 10 minutes, and add the mushrooms to the leeks, stirring to combine. Add the flour and cook for 1 minute. Add the vegetable stock, wine, and salt and pepper to taste. Bring the mixture to a boil, immediately reduce the heat, and simmer for 15 to 20 minutes.

Add the cream, half and half and the parsley. Season with more salt and pepper, if needed, and heat the soup through. Do NOT allow it to boil. Serve the soup hot, and garnish each serving with a pinch of parsley and a splash of truffle oil. Bon Appetito!

SALADS & SIDES

Rouge et Noir Brie Quiche

Seared Pork Tenderloin with Rocket-Chicory Salad

'Baked Comfort' Tomato Bread Pudding

BALLETTO VINEYARDS

Once again, we are proud to serve an innovative dish prepared by chef Roger Praplan of La Gare Restaurant in Santa Rosa. This small, family-owned establishment has been a Sonoma County favorite for more than 30 years, and uses fresh local ingredients to create both traditional and contemporary French dishes. For this quiche, try using Rouge et Noir Brie from the Marin French Cheese Co., which despite its name, is located in Petaluma in Sonoma County.

5700 Occidental Road
Santa Rosa, CA 05401
707-568-2455
ballettovineyards.com

rouge et noir
BRIE QUICHE
chef Roger Praplan, La Gare Restaurant

vegi

Pair with Balletto Estate Chardonnay

SERVES 8-10
8-inch pie shell
6 ounces Brie cheese, rind on
3/4 cup half and half
salt and white pepper
pinch freshly ground nutmeg
3 egg yolks
2 whole eggs
2 teaspoons chives, finely chopped
3/4 cup heavy cream

Bake an 8-inch pie shell at 350° until it's light gold in color. Leave the oven on.

In a blender or food processor, place the Brie and half and half and process them to a smooth consistency. Add a dash of salt, white pepper and nutmeg, and blend again.

Quickly add the eggs with the chives and do not overwork. Add the cream last. When blended, place the mixture in the prebaked pie shell. Place the quiche on a sheet pan and set it on a rack in the middle of the oven. Let it bake slowly, as it has a different texture than a classic cheese and ham quiche. If it browns too rapidly, cover the quiche with aluminum foil and lower the temperature. Cooking time is 45 to 55 minutes, or until the quiche sets to a firm touch.

RUSSIAN RIVER VINEYARDS

The beauty of this dish is that it can serve as an appetizer, a substantial salad, or an entrée, depending on portion size. I've scaled this recipe as a salad course. For the vinaigrette, I like to use Banyuls, a French vinegar made from wine grapes; you can also use good-quality Sherry vinegar that is 5% acidity; look on the label for the percentage.

5700 Gravenstein Highway North
Forestville, CA 95436
707-887-3344
russianrivervineyards.com

SEARED PORK TENDERLOIN
with rocket-chicory salad

chef Todd Davies

Pair with Russian River Vineyards Pinot Noir

SERVES 4

1 pork tenderloin, silver
 skin removed
kosher salt
black pepper
1/4 cup canola or olive oil
4 ounces Pinot Noir
1-1/2 ounces dried cranberries
1/2 teaspoon Dijon mustard
2 teaspoons shallots, minced
1 tablespoon Banyuls vinegar
1/4 cup olive oil
1/2 teaspoon kosher salt
1/4 teaspoon black pepper,
 coarse ground
2 ounces rocket (baby
 arugula)
2 ounces chicory (frisée),
 cleaned

Preheat oven to 350°.

Season the pork tenderloin liberally with salt and pepper. Cut it in half, if necessary, so that it will fit into a sauté pan.

Heat the 1/4 cup canola or olive oil in an ovenproof sauté pan and carefully place the tenderloin into the hot oil. Sear the pork on all sides, so that it is evenly caramelized. Place the pan in the oven and cook the tenderloin to medium, or approximately 155° as gauged by a meat thermometer.

While the pork cooks, bring the Pinot Noir and dried cranberries to a boil in a small pan and then remove it from the heat.

To prepare the salad, place the Dijon mustard, shallots, vinegar, olive oil, kosher salt and black pepper in a small bowl and mix with a fork until the vinaigrette is slightly emulsified. Place the rocket and frisée lettuces in a large bowl and toss with the vinaigrette.

To serve, place a mound of salad onto 4 plates. Slice the pork and fan out the slices at the base of the salads. Garnish with the Pinot Noir-plumped cranberries.

TOPEL WINERY TASTING ROOM

Every year, I grow TOO many tomatoes, and end up preserving, drying and roasting them, and making sauces that last almost all the way through winter. Guests who visit us from late fall through winter look forward to a few mainstays coming out of our wood-fired oven: roasted chicken, lamb or beef, and this homey bread pudding. I adapted the recipe for regular home ovens — and it's scrumptious!

125 Matheson Street
Healdsburg, CA 95448
707-433-4116
topelwines.com

'baked comfort' tomato
BREAD PUDDING

chef Donnis Topel

Pair with Topel Estate Reserve Cabernet Sauvignon

SERVES 8

3 pounds plum tomatoes, halved lengthwise

1-1/4 teaspoons herbs de Provence

1/2 cup extra-virgin olive oil

3/4 teaspoon salt

1/2 teaspoon black pepper

1 head garlic, left whole

10 cups cubed (1-inch) rustic sourdough-style bread

2 cups whole milk

1 cup heavy cream

8 large eggs

2 teaspoons salt

1-1/2 teaspoons pepper

2 cups chilled Fontina cheese, coarsely grated

1/2 cup Parmigiano-Reggiano cheese, grated

Preheat oven to 400°.

Butter a 13-inch by 9-inch shallow baking dish.

Toss the tomatoes in a large bowl with the herbs de Provence, 1 tablespoon of the olive oil, and the salt and pepper. Arrange the tomatoes, cut side up, on 1 of 2 large, heavy-rimmed baking sheets.

Cut off and discard 1/4-inch from the top of the garlic head to expose the cloves. Put the garlic on a sheet of foil and drizzle it with 1 teaspoon of olive oil. Wrap the garlic head in the foil and roast in the baking dish with the tomatoes until the tomatoes are browned but still juicy, and the garlic is soft, 50 to 60 minutes. Leave the oven on.

Let the garlic cool to slightly warm to the touch. Using a rubber spatula, push the garlic through a medium-mesh sieve. Discard the garlic skin and reserve the puree.

While the garlic cools, toss the bread cubes in a large bowl with the remaining olive oil, and spread the bread out on the second rimmed baking sheet; bake until golden brown, 20 to 25 minutes. Let the bread cool in the pan.

Reduce the oven temperature to 350°.

In a large bowl, whisk together the garlic puree, milk, cream, eggs, salt and pepper. Stir in the grated cheeses. Transfer the bread cubes to a baking dish, then pour the egg mixture over the bread and add the tomatoes, pushing some down between the bread cubes. Bake until firm to the touch and golden brown in spots, 50 to 60 minutes, and serve.

PASTA & RICE

Risotto Amista

Baked Rigatoni with Olives & Sausage

Spaghetti with Meat Sauce

Risotto with Roasted Cippolini, Portobellos & Rainbow Chard

Spring Hill Mac & Cheese with Bacon

Lemon Risotto

Mushroom Ragout

Cannelloni con Spinaci e Salmone

Peppery Pancetta Pasta

Risotto al Radicchio Rosso

Bill's Bolognese

Diane's Baked Penne Pasta

AMISTA VINEYARDS

Chardonnay? We grow it but never planned to make it...until our friends insisted. A Dry Creek Valley winemaker showed us a style we could love — one that lets the fruit shine. Now we have the perfect wine to drink with one of our all-time favorites, risotto. But this is no ordinary risotto. Chef John Franchetti adds special touches, such as lightly sautéed shrimp and a dollop of creamy mascarpone, and tops it with a salad of arugula and oyster mushrooms. This is a dish to make with friends, so you can take turns stirring, sipping and enjoying the good life.

3320 Dry Creek Road
Healdsburg, CA 95448
707-431-9200
amistavineyards.com

RISOTTO AMISTA

chef John Franchetti, Rosso Pizzeria

Pair with Amista Dry Creek Valley Chardonnay

SERVES 8

SHRIMP STOCK
Shells from 2 pounds medium shrimp
   (deveined); reserve shrimp meat
6 bay leaves
1 ounce black peppercorns
3 ounces Amista Chardonnay
1 gallon water

RISOTTO
3 tablespoons extra-virgin olive oil
1/4 cup carrots, chopped
1/4 cup celery, chopped
3/4 cup onion, chopped
salt and pepper
2-1/3 cups Arborio rice
1/2 bottle Amista Chardonnay
1-1/2 gallons shrimp stock
2 bunches green onions, thinly sliced
1/2 cup mascarpone cheese
2 tablespoons Parmesan cheese, grated

MUSHROOM SALAD
1 tablespoon extra-virgin olive oil
2 cloves garlic, chopped
1/4 pound (1 stick) butter
1-1/2 pounds abalone or oyster
   mushrooms, thinly sliced
1/2 bunch parsley, chopped
salt and pepper
1/2 pound arugula
1 tablespoon freshly squeezed
   lemon juice

First prepare the shrimp stock. Add all the ingredients to a large stockpot and bring to a boil, then reduce the heat to simmer. Simmer for 30 minutes. Allow the stock to cool, then strain out and discard the solids.

To prepare the risotto, heat 1 tablespoon of olive oil in a large stockpot over medium heat. Add the carrots, celery and onion and season with salt and pepper. Sauté the vegetables for 4 minutes. Stir in the rice and season with more salt and pepper. Add the wine and stir continuously until all the liquid is absorbed. Add the shrimp stock 1/2 quart at a time, stirring each addition until the liquid is absorbed by the rice. Continue adding stock and stirring until the rice is tender (there will be leftover stock). Season with salt and pepper to taste, and stir in the green onions. Spread the mascarpone on a serving dish and top with the risotto.

In a large sauté pan, heat the remaining 2 tablespoons of olive oil over medium heat. Add the reserved shrimp meat and season with salt and pepper. Sauté the shrimp, stirring constantly, until they are cooked through, about 4 minutes. Place the shrimp on top of the risotto and keep warm until ready to serve.

To prepare the salad, preheat the oven to 350°. In a large ovenproof sauté pan, heat 1 tablespoon of olive oil over medium heat. Add the garlic and sauté until it's tender. Add the butter and stir until melted. Add the mushrooms and parsley, season with salt and pepper, and stir to coat with the butter mixture. Bake in the oven for 8 minutes. In a bowl, toss the arugula with the mushroom mixture and lemon juice. Spoon the salad on top of the risotto and garnish with Parmesan and a drizzle of extra-virgin olive oil.

CELLARS OF SONOMA

Jack Mitchell's restaurant is located a few doors down from our tasting room. Our guests can order lunch or dinner to enjoy in the tasting room with the wines of our boutique producers. Jack's Baked Rigatoni was made for Zinfandel!

133 4th Street
Santa Rosa, CA 95401
707-578-1826
cellarsofsonoma.com

BAKED RIGATONI
with olives & sausage

chef Jack Mitchell, Jack and Tony's Restaurant & Whiskey Bar

Pair with Gann Family Cellars Zinfandel

SERVES 6

1 pound rigatoni, ziti or
  penne pasta
1 pound sweet or spicy
  Italian sausage
½ onion, diced
½ cup oil-cured olives,
  pitted and halved
1 cup chicken stock
4 tablespoons tomato paste
1 tablespoon dry oregano
2 tablespoons garlic,
  chopped
1 bunch parsley, chopped
1 ounce Vella Dry Jack
  cheese, grated

Preheat oven to 350°.

Cook the pasta according to package instructions; it should be al dente, or slightly firm to the bite.

Crumble the sausage into a large sauté pan and cook it over medium heat until the meat loses its pink color. Add the onion, olives, chicken stock, tomato paste, oregano and garlic and continue to cook, until the vegetables are tender. Remove the pan from the heat.

Add the cooked pasta to the pan, stir to coat the pasta with the sauce, and pour the mixture into an ovenproof baking dish. Sprinkle the top with the cheese and bake the pasta for approximately 20 minutes, until the top is bubbly and beginning to form a crust. Add chopped parsley to finish, and serve.

CLOS DU BOIS WINERY

This recipe was created by celebrity chef Katie Lee as one of her winter go-to recipes. It pairs perfectly with Clos du Bois Old Vine Zinfandel and is a staff favorite.

19410 Geyserville Avenue
Geyserville, CA 95441
800-222-3189
closdubois.com

SPAGHETTI
with meat sauce

Recipe by Katie Lee

Pair with Clos du Bois Old Vine Zinfandel

SERVES 4-6

2 pounds lean ground beef

1 onion, peeled and grated

1 12-ounce can tomato paste

1 16-ounce can tomato sauce

2 cups water

2 tablespoons sugar

2 tablespoons chili powder

1 teaspoon garlic salt

1-$\frac{1}{2}$ teaspoons salt

1 teaspoon freshly ground
   black pepper

2 bay leaves

1 tablespoon white wine
   vinegar

1 pound spaghetti

grated Parmesan cheese,
   for serving

In a large stockpot or Dutch oven, combine the beef (do not brown it first), grated onion, tomato paste, tomato sauce, water, sugar, chili powder, garlic salt, salt and pepper. Mix until the ingredients are combined.

Add the bay leaves, cover the pot and simmer over medium-low heat for approximately 2 hours. Stir in the white wine vinegar and simmer another 30 minutes.

Bring a large pot of salted water to a boil. Add the spaghetti and cook until it's al dente. Drain the pasta in a colander and place in a large serving bowl. To serve, toss the spaghetti with the sauce, and sprinkle the grated Parmesan cheese over the top.

DRAXTON WINES

When chef Ken Rochioli and I discussed what to serve for the event, we ran through several options. We both wanted something in the "comfort food" arena, and we wanted to feature our 2010 Russian River Valley Pinot Noir. After making a list and whittling it down, we decided that risotto definitely fit the bill. The earthiness of the portobello mushrooms and the aromas of the Pinot were a perfect match. We hope you agree.

4001 Highway 128
Geyserville, CA 95441
707-857-3300
draxtonwines.com

RISOTTO
with roasted cippolini, portobellos & rainbow chard

chef Ken Rochioli, KR Catering

Pair with Draxton Heliodoro Russian River Valley Pinot Noir

SERVES 4-6

8 ounces cippolini onions

3 tablespoons olive oil

kosher salt and freshly
    ground pepper

1 tablespoon unsalted butter

1/2 pound portobello
    mushrooms, diced

1/2 cup yellow onions,
    chopped

1/2 cup Arborio rice

1 tablespoon fresh thyme,
    chopped

1/2 cup Draxton Russian River
    Valley Pinot Noir

5 cups hot chicken stock

1-3/4 cups loosely packed
    rainbow chard, chopped

1 cup tomatoes, seeded and
    chopped

3/4 cup Parmesan cheese,
    grated

Preheat the oven to 350°.

Trim the ends of the cippolini onions, and peel off the outer layer (discard). Slice the onions in half, coat them with 1 tablespoon of olive oil, and sprinkle them lightly with salt and pepper. Wrap the onions loosely in foil and roast them in the oven for 65 minutes. Keep them wrapped in foil until serving time.

In a large sauté pan over medium heat, heat remaining 2 tablespoons of olive oil and the butter. Add the mushrooms and yellow onions and sauté for 3 minutes, stirring frequently. Add the rice and thyme and continue cooking for 5 minutes, stirring frequently. Carefully add the wine (it may steam up when poured into the hot pan) and simmer to evaporate the liquid. Start adding the chicken stock in 1/2-cup increments, slowly stirring until most of the liquid has evaporated. Continue to add stock and stir until the rice is al dente.

Stir in the chard and tomatoes. Cook for 1 to 2 minutes more to wilt the chard slightly. Stir in the Parmesan and garnish with the cippolini onions.

HOLDREDGE WINES

Certain points in life are beyond dispute: (1) Simple is better, and (2) bacon makes *everything* better. Not a lot of foods are simpler than mac and cheese — it's the poster child for comfort food. But when you add in (as we love to do) bacon, well, it just doesn't get much better — unless you pair that with Pinot Noir, as we like to do. This recipe is the convergence of those two indisputable truths.

51 Front Street
Healdsburg, CA 95448
(707) 431-1424
holdredge.com

spring hill
MAC & CHEESE WITH BACON

chef Ken Rochioli, KR Catering

Pair with Holdredge Russian River Valley Pinot Noir

SERVES 6
HERBED BREAD CRUMBS
1-1/2 cups panko bread crumbs,
    unflavored
1 teaspoon unsalted butter,
    softened
1/2 teaspoon fresh thyme, chopped
1/2 teaspoon fresh oregano, chopped
1/2 teaspoon kosher salt
1/8 teaspoon ground black pepper

MAC & CHEESE
3/4 pound bacon, diced
3 tablespoons salted butter
1/2 cup all-purpose flour
1/2 cup dry white wine
5 cups whole milk, room
    temperature
1-1/4 cups heavy cream
1 pound Spring Hill white Cheddar,
    grated (medium-aged, not overly
    sharp)
1-1/4 teaspoons Colman's dry
    mustard
1/2 teaspoon white pepper, fine grind
3 teaspoons kosher salt
6 cups elbow macaroni, cooked
1-1/2 cups herbed bread crumbs
    (see above recipe)

To prepare the bread crumbs, combine all the ingredients in a bowl and set aside. To prepare the macaroni, place the bacon in a heavy-bottomed saucepan over medium heat. Cover the pan and cook the bacon, stirring occasionally until it's crisp. Save 2 tablespoons of bacon fat and remove the bacon from the pan. Reserve the bacon and the fat.

Melt the butter and add the flour in a clean heavy-bottomed saucepan. Stir and cook the roux over low-medium heat for 10 minutes, making sure it doesn't brown. Allow the roux to cool slightly. Add the white wine and 1/2 cup of milk into the butter-flour mixture and mix until smooth. Add another 1/2 cup of milk and stir again until smooth. Increase the heat to medium and slowly stir in the rest of the milk and all of the cream, to ensure you have no lumps. Stir the mixture and bring it to a simmer; it should thicken as it cooks. Make sure you stir in the corners and bottom of the pan to prevent burning. Simmer for at least 20 minutes, until the mixture is smooth and silky. If it has any lumps, strain it and return it to the stove over medium-low heat.

Preheat the oven to 375°.

Add the cheese, dry mustard, bacon, bacon fat and white pepper, and stir. Add half of the salt and taste for seasoning; add the rest of the salt if needed. Remove the pan from the heat and add the cooked macaroni to the cheese sauce, stirring to combine. Pour the macaroni into a 9-inch by 9-inch ceramic baking dish, top with the bread crumbs, and brown the mac and cheese in the oven, until it's bubbling hot and crispy-golden on top.

INSPIRATION VINEYARDS

Inspired by wonderful flavors and pure simplicity, this recipe is a family favorite year-round. The secret to making creamy risotto is slow and constant stirring. What we like most about this recipe is that it can be used as a base for many variations. For example, the addition of fresh thyme creates a more savory dish that is a wonderful accompaniment with roasted chicken. We also like to add bay scallops at the end, turning this recipe into a complete entrée.

3360 Coffey Lane, Suite E
Santa Rosa, CA 95401
707-237-4980
inspirationvineyards.com

LEMON RISOTTO

chef Bruce Riezenman, Park Avenue Catering

Pair with Inspiration Vineyards Estate Chardonnay

SERVES 4

3-1/2 cups low-sodium chicken broth

1 tablespoon extra-virgin olive oil

1 medium onion, minced

4 cloves garlic, minced

1 cup Arborio rice

1 cup Inspiration 2010 Estate Chardonnay

zest of 1 lemon

1 tablespoon fresh lemon juice

1/4 cup fresh-grated Parmesan cheese

In a saucepan, bring the chicken broth to a simmer and leave it on low heat.

In a large frying pan over medium-high heat, add the olive oil, onion and garlic, and gently sauté them until they're translucent. Add the rice and sauté until warm, stirring constantly. Add the wine and cook until almost all of the wine has been absorbed.

Add 1/2 cup of warm chicken broth, the lemon zest and lemon juice, stirring constantly until most of the liquid is absorbed. Continue adding 1/2 cup of broth at a time, stirring constantly while the broth is absorbed, until there is only 1/2 cup of broth remaining. Stir the final 1/2 cup of broth into the rice and stir.

For a richer dish, add 1 pound of bay scallops as you add final 1/2 cup of broth. The scallops take only a few minutes to cook, so be sure to remove the pan from the heat shortly after you make this addition. Stir in the Parmesan and serve.

MARTIN RAY WINERY

This is a great dish to serve with pasta or soft polenta. Trumpet Royale mushrooms, grown by Gourmet Mushrooms in Sebastopol, have a rich, savory character that bridges the aromas and flavors of our Pinot Noir.

2191 Laguna Road
Santa Rosa, CA 95401
707-823-2404
martinraywinery.com

MUSHROOM RAGOUT

vegi

chef Bruce Riezenman, Park Avenue Catering

Pair with Martin Ray Russian River Valley Pinot Noir

SERVES 8

1 quart fresh tomatoes,
   cut into wedges
2 tablespoons extra-virgin
   olive oil
1/2 medium yellow onion,
   finely diced
2 bay leaves
1/8 teaspoon dried red pepper
   flakes
1 cup Trumpet Royale
   mushrooms, roughly
   chopped
1 cup shiitake mushrooms,
   quartered
1/8 ounce (by weight) dried
   porcini mushrooms,
   chopped
1 cup Martin Ray Pinot Noir
1 tablespoon fine red wine
   vinegar
1/2 cup Grana Padano cheese,
   grated
1/4 cup fresh basil,
   finely slivered
salt and pepper

In a small bowl, toss the tomato wedges with salt and let them sit for 20 minutes.

Add the olive oil to a sauté pan, add the onions and let them cook, covered, over medium heat. When the onions are soft, add the bay leaves, red pepper flakes and mushrooms. Stir, cover and cook for 10 minutes to soften the onions, stirring occasionally.

Add the wine and reduce the mixture over high heat until it's almost dry. Add the tomatoes and vinegar, stir, reduce the heat and let the mixture simmer, covered, for 20 minutes. Add salt as needed.

Place the mushroom mixture in a food processor and pulse until it is chopped the coarse texture of a ragout. Once the ragout has cooled, add the cheese and basil.

Reheat the dish and serve it over soft polenta or toss with pasta. If needed, thin it slightly with water or chicken broth.

PORTALUPI WINE

Says Jane Portalupi: My husband (and winemaker for Portalupi) smokes the salmon in our backyard using the "Mother of all Smokehouses" built by Tim Portalupi and his father, Tony. It's the brine that makes this so special! Tim loves talking about smoking meats and fish; if you want the family brine recipe, please contact us.

107 North Street
Healdsburg, CA 95448
707-395-0960
portalupiwine.com

CANNELLONI
con spinaci e salmone
(spinach & salmon)

chef Tim Vallery, Peloton Catering

Pair with Portalupi Pinot Noir

SERVES 6

SAUCE
6 tablespoons butter
   or margarine
6 tablespoons flour
1-1/2 cups whole milk
1-1/2 cups chicken stock
3/4 cup clam juice
1/4 teaspoon salt
1/4 teaspoon ground nutmeg
1/4 teaspoon white pepper
1/4 teaspoon cayenne

FILLING
1-1/2 pounds smoked salmon fillet
4 cups fresh spinach, washed,
   stems removed
2 tablespoons Luna Portalupi
   Rosemary Olive Oil
1/2 cup onion, chopped
2 cloves garlic, minced
2 large lightly beaten eggs
2 tablespoons dry bread crumbs
12 cannelloni shells
1/2 cup heavy cream
1/3 cup grated Parmesan cheese
2 lemon wedges

Preheat oven to 325°.

To prepare the sauce, melt the butter in a large saucepan over medium heat. Add the flour and cook the roux without allowing it to brown, whisking often, for 2 minutes. Add the milk, chicken stock and clam juice. Season with the salt, nutmeg, white pepper and cayenne. Cook, whisking constantly, until the sauce thickens. Remove the pan from the heat as soon as the sauce boils.

To prepare the filling, remove the skin from the smoked salmon and crumble the fillet into a large bowl. Chop the spinach coarsely and cook, uncovered, in a large pan with 1-inch of water for 3 to 4 minutes. Drain the spinach and squeeze out as much liquid as possible. Add the spinach to the salmon.

Add the rosemary olive oil to a small sauté pan over medium heat. Add the onion and sauté until it's soft, about 5 minutes. Add the garlic and sauté 2 minutes. Add the onion-garlic mixture to the salmon mixture, then add the eggs, bread crumbs and 1 cup of the sauce. Stir to combine.

Cook the cannelloni according to package directions. Drain the pasta and plunge it into a bowl of cold water, then drain again.

To assemble the cannelloni, coat the bottom of 2 9-inch by 13-inch baking dishes with 1/4 cup each of heavy cream. Using a large pastry bag, pipe the filling into the cannelloni shells. Place 6 filled shells into each baking dish. Spoon the remaining sauce evenly over the cannelloni and sprinkle them with the Parmesan. Cover the dishes with foil and bake 30 minutes. Remove the foil and bake for 15 more minutes. Squeeze fresh lemon juice over the top of each dish and serve immediately.

SODA ROCK WINERY

Nothing beats comfort food, and this dish is the definition of it. Although it is a very simple recipe, it will truly impress your friends and family. The first three steps, through cooking the pasta, can be done a day in advance.

8015 Highway 128
Healdsburg, CA 95448
707-433-3303
sodarockwinery.com

peppery
PANCETTA PASTA

chef Ryan Waldron

Pair with Soda Rock Winery Cabernet Franc

SERVES 4-6

2 red bell peppers

2 yellow bell peppers

1 pound asparagus spears

2 tablespoons olive oil

1 tablespoon balsamic vinegar

2 tablespoons salt

3/4 pound penne pasta

4 tablespoons unsalted
   butter

3 ounces pancetta, diced

1 teaspoon minced garlic

1-1/2 cups chicken stock

1-1/2 tablespoons fresh thyme,
   minced

2/3 cups Parmesan cheese,
   grated

kosher salt and freshly
   ground pepper

Preheat the oven to broil.

Cut the bell peppers in half, removed the seeds and stems, and place them skin side up under broiler, allowing them to become charred and blistered. Place them in a bowl, cover with plastic wrap and let the peppers cool for 10 minutes. Remove the blistered skin and dice the peppers.

Heat a barbecue grill to hot. Toss the asparagus with the olive oil and balsamic vinegar. Place the spears on the grill, rotating them as needed to caramelize but not fully cook them. Let the asparagus cool and cut the spears into 1-inch pieces.

Bring a large pot of water and 2 tablespoons of salt to a boil. Add the pasta and cook until it's al dente, about 7 to 8 minutes. Drain the pasta. If you make this a day advance, run cold water over the pasta to stop it from cooking.

In a large skillet, melt 2 tablespoons of the butter over medium heat. Add the pancetta and cook until it's lightly crisp on the edges. Add the asparagus, peppers and garlic and toss for 1 minute. Add the stock and bring the mixture to a boil. Add the pasta and thyme and stir well to combine; cook for 6 to 7 minutes, keeping the pasta al dente.

To finish, add 1/2 of the Parmesan and the remaining 2 tablespoons of butter. Season to taste with salt and pepper. Garnish with the remaining cheese and serve immediately.

TWOMEY CELLARS

The key to risotto is constant stirring. We mean this literally: Constant agitation and stirring causes the starch to dissolve away from the rice grains and blend into the sauce, creating the creamy texture of the risotto. The risotto in this recipe takes on a beautiful rose color from the addition of red wine instead of white wine. The bacon is optional, but I find it adds an essential umami characteristic. The radicchio provides a wonderful bitter taste that is balanced by the sweet balsamic.

3000 Westside Road
Healdsburg, CA 95448
707-942-7120
twomeycellars.com

RISOTTO AL RADICCHIO

rosso

chef Dominic Orsini

Pair with Twomey Russian River Valley Pinot Noir

SERVES 4-6

1 teaspoon olive oil

6 slices bacon, diced small (optional)

½ cup red onion, diced small

1 tablespoon garlic, chopped

2 cups Carnaroli or Arborio rice

1 cup Pinot Noir

1 tablespoon salt

10 cups vegetable or chicken broth, held hot in saucepot

1 head radicchio, cut into bite-size pieces

1 cup Vella Dry Jack cheese, grated (or Parmesan)

¼ cup extra-virgin olive oil

2 tablespoons aged balsamic vinegar

Place a 1-gallon saucepot over medium heat. When it's fully heated, add the olive oil and the bacon. Cook the bacon for 10 to 15 minutes until it's brown and crispy, stirring often.

Add the onion and garlic; cook for an additional 3 minutes, stirring often. Add the rice and cook for an additional 3 minutes, stirring often. Add the wine and salt, and bring the wine to a simmer. From this point on, you must constantly stir the rice so that it doesn't burn or overcook.

When the wine is fully absorbed into the rice, stir in 1 cup of broth. Continue to stir constantly until all of the broth is absorbed into the rice. Repeat this step until only 2 cups of the broth are left.

Taste the risotto, biting into the individual rice grains. The rice should be firm yet give all the way to the center. If there is still a tiny bit of raw grain in the center of the mixture, continue adding broth. The risotto should be creamy and pourable; if it doesn't pour off your spoon, add more broth or water until it does.

Stir in the radicchio and the cheese. Taste the rice and adjust the seasoning and/or acidity; if the risotto seems bland, your wine might not have enough acidity. If this is the case, squeeze lemon juice into the rice.

Spoon the risotto onto a platter and drizzle it with extra-virgin olive oil and balsamic vinegar

WHITE OAK VINEYARDS & WINERY

When returning from his long and cold fishing adventures in Alaska, White Oak founder/owner Bill Meyers always looks forward to a hot plate of friend and neighbor Dan Lucia's Pasta Bolognese!

7505 Highway 128
Healdsburg, CA 95448
707-433-8429
whiteoakwinery.com

BILL'S BOLOGNESE

chef Dan Lucia

Pair with White Oak Syrah

SERVES 6-8

3 tablespoons olive oil
3 tablespoons butter
1 cup onions, diced
3 cloves garlic, minced
1/2 cup carrots, diced
1/2 cup celery, diced
2 tablespoons parsley,
   chopped
1-1/2 pounds ground beef
   chuck
1-1/2 pounds ground pork
1 cup White Oak Chardonnay
1 cup milk
1 cup tomato puree
2-1/2 cups beef broth
1 cup heavy cream
salt and pepper to taste
1 teaspoon nutmeg

In a heavy-bottom saucepot, heat the oil and butter. Add the onions, garlic, carrots, celery and parsley, and saute on low heat for about 10 minutes, or until the vegetables are tender.

Add the meats and cook until they are golden brown, about 20 minutes. Add the wine and reduce it by half. Add the milk, tomato puree and beef broth. Simmer on low heat for 1 hour or more, until the sauce is thick. Add the cream and nutmeg, and simmer for 10 more minutes.

Serve hot over your favorite pasta.

WILSON WINERY

Feel free to use your own favorite tomato sauce for this hearty dish, or follow the recipe here; it can be made up to 5 days ahead and refrigerated. Prepare the béchamel sauce just before you begin to cook the pasta.

1960 Dry Creek Road
Healdsburg, CA 95448
707-433-4355
wilsonwinery.com

diane's
BAKED PENNE PASTA

chef Diane Wilson

Pair with Wilson Molly's Vineyard Dry Creek Valley Zinfandel

SERVES 6-8

BÉCHAMEL SAUCE

5 tablespoons butter

3 tablespoons all-purpose flour

2 cups milk

2 teaspoons salt

$\frac{1}{2}$ teaspoon nutmeg, freshly grated

TOMATO SAUCE

1 onion

4 garlic cloves

1 medium carrot, finely shredded

4 tablespoons olive oil or fat
  reserved from bacon

1 28-ounce can crushed tomatoes

4 tablespoons basil, finely chopped

$\frac{1}{2}$ teaspoon crushed red pepper
  flakes

BAKED PENNE

1 pound mini penne pasta

2 cups tomato sauce

2 cups béchamel sauce

$\frac{1}{2}$ pound cooked bacon, diced

$\frac{1}{2}$ cup basil, chopped

1 pound fresh mozzarella, cut into
  cubes

$\frac{3}{4}$ pound Fontina cheese, shredded

$\frac{1}{2}$ cup Parmigiano Reggiano cheese,
  grated

$\frac{3}{4}$ cup panko bread crumbs

To prepare the béchemel sauce, in a medium saucepan, heat the butter over medium-low heat until it's melted. Add the flour and stir to get a smooth consistency. Cook the roux over medium heat until the mixture is lightly golden, about 3 to 4 minutes. Warm the milk and add it slowly to the butter mixture, whisking continuously until very smooth. Bring the mixture to a simmer and cook for 10 minutes, stirring constantly. Remove the pan from the heat and season the sauce with salt and nutmeg. Set aside.

To prepare the tomato sauce, sauté the onion, garlic and carrot in the olive oil over medium heat until the vegetables are translucent but not brown (about 10 minutes). Add the tomatoes, bring the mixture to a boil, lower the heat to just bubbling, and cook for 30 to 40 minutes, stirring occasionally. Add the basil and crushed red pepper flakes and cook 5 minutes more. Season with salt and pepper to taste.

Preheat oven to 375°.

Cook the penne according to the package instructions. Drain the pasta, refresh it in cold water, and place it in a large mixing bowl. Add the tomato sauce, béchamel sauce, bacon, basil, mozzarella and grated cheeses and stir to mix well. Pour the pasta into a baking dish, sprinkle the top with the bread crumbs, and bake until it is bubbling and crusty on top, about 30 to 40 minutes. Serve immediately.

ENTRÉES

Chicken Ragout with Soft Polenta

Sausage & Mushroom Ragout

French Dip Sliders with Karma Au Jus

Mom's Sunday Sauce with
Sausages & Meatballs

Spiedini d' Loiodice con Polenta Enrico

Pollo a la Catalana

Roasted Pork Shoulder with Dried Cherry, Bacon
& Sweet Onion Compote

Moroccan Lamb Stew with Tart Cherries

Rustic Restaurant Marrakesh Lamb

Zin-Braised Beef

St. George & Bacon Grilled Cheese with
Caramelized Onions & Herb Aioli

Sicilian Lamb Meatballs

Not So Traditional Osso Buco with Gremolata

Lip-Smackin' Baby Back Ribs

Chicken Marbella

Cuban Pork Stew with Sweet Potato Mash

Red Wine-Braised Short Ribs with
Truffled Celery Root Puree

Kobe Tri-Tip Sandwiches with
Cabernet-Braised Cabbage & Blue
Cheese-Buttermilk Dressing

Osso Buco Stew with Gremolata &
Freeze-Dried Corn

Sausage Skewers with Mushrooms &
Syrah Dipping Sauce

Coq au Vin

Wild Boar Sausage

Oxtail & Short Rib Ragu over Soft Polenta

Soul Surfer Ribs

It's Just Pork ... and Chutney

Turkey & White Bean Chili

New Contadina

Wild Game Stew

Duck & Pork Cassoulet

Beef Ribs with Zinfandel-Maple Reduction Sauce

Josh Silvers' Drunken Duck

Nonna's Italian Meatballs

Roast Duck Bread Pudding

Duck Confit with Emily's Cuvée Reduction &
Creamy Polenta

Meatloaf with Pancetta & Shiitake Mushrooms

Pork & Pancetta Pot Pie

Chicken & Sausage Jambalaya

Ricotta Malfatti with Sweet Italian Sausage,
Spinach & Peppers

Margherita Pizza

South African-Style Boerewors Sausages with
Merlot-Caramelized Onions

Braised Pork Shank with Apricots

Spinach & Portobello Mushroom Lasagne

Provencal Lamb Daube with Red Wine,
Olives & Oranges

Steak Sapphire with Sautéed Spinach,
Crab & Béarnaise Sauce

Creole Lobster

Petite Ribs & Celariac Puree

Frane's Mom's Bakalar

Sriracha Chicken

Smokin' Pulled Pork Sliders with
Cider Vinegar Sauce

Kissable Baked Polenta with Pinot Noir-Braised
Wild Mushrooms

Cabernet-Braised Short Ribs

Rockin' Rattler Pork & Beef Sugo over Polenta

Mesquite-Charred Bistro Steak with
Zinfandel Reduction & Pilaf

Grilled Skirt Steak with Chimi Sauce

Korean-Style Braised Short Rib
Rice Bowl with Kimchi

ALDERBROOK WINERY

This recipe is a favorite of winemaker Bryan Parker and his production crew; we serve it every year during harvest. It's a great match with our Carignane (kah-ree-NYAHN), a variety that originated in the Carinena district of Spain. At one time Carignane was widely planted in California, but its popularity has waned. With limited amounts of well-grown Carignane available in Sonoma County, we are fortunate to have access to an old-vine vineyard in Dry Creek Valley, specifically School House Creek Vineyard.

2306 Magnolia Drive
Healdsburg, CA
707-433-5987
alderbrook.com harvest

CHICKEN RAGOUT
with soft polenta

chef Dan Lucia

Pair with Alderbrook Carignane

SERVES 6-8

RAGOUT
⅓ cup olive oil
8 boneless, skinless chicken
  thighs, cut in half
2 skinless chicken breasts,
  cut into cubes
2 cups crimini mushrooms,
  sliced
1 yellow onion, diced
5 cloves garlic, minced
3 stalks celery, sliced
4 carrots, diced
1 12-ounce can diced tomatoes
3 tablespoons fresh thyme
½ teaspoon red pepper flakes
6 cups chicken stock
salt and pepper to taste
1 cup Parmesan cheese, grated

POLENTA
6 cups chicken stock or water
2 cups heavy cream
4 gloves garlic, minced
3 cups polenta
½ cup butter
salt and pepper to taste

To prepare the ragout, in a large sauté pan, heat half of the olive oil and sear the chicken pieces until they're golden brown. Remove the chicken from the pan and set aside.

In a large stock pot, heat the remaining olive oil and add the mushrooms. Sauté for 5 minutes. Add the onions, garlic, celery and carrots and continue to cook for approximately 6 minutes. Add the browned chicken, tomatoes, thyme, red pepper flakes and chicken stock. Bring the mixture to a low simmer, cover the pot and cook the ragout slowly for 1 hour. Season with salt and pepper.

To prepare the polenta, in a heavy-bottom stockpot, add the stock and cream. Bring the liquid to a simmer and add the garlic and polenta. With a whisk, slowly stir the polenta until it's soft and creamy. Whisk in the butter and season with salt and pepper.

Serve the ragout over the polenta and garnish with the grated Parmesan.

ALEXANDER VALLEY VINEYARDS

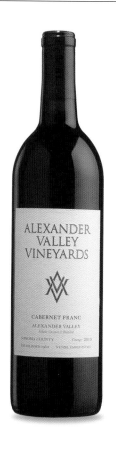

AVV assistant winemaker Harry Wetzel grew up surrounded by the family's estate vineyards and gardens. He fondly remembers his grandmother, Maggie Wetzel, cooking for family and friends and using fresh vegetables and herbs from her garden. "Her cooking was a big inspiration to me," Harry recalls. "I grew to appreciate the amount of time, love and effort that went into her creations, and so I see cooking for my friends and family as an extension of that."

8644 Highway 128
Healdsburg, CA 95448
707-433-7209
avvwine.com

sausage & mushroom

RAGOUT

chef Harry Wetzel IV

Pair with Alexander Valley Vineyards Estate Cabernet Franc

SERVES 4-6

1 tablespoon butter, softened

1-1/2 teaspoons flour

1 pound mild Italian sausage (either bulk, or removed from casings)

1 teaspoon olive oil

1 medium onion, chopped

2 stalks celery, chopped

2 carrots, chopped

1/2 teaspoon red pepper flakes

1 teaspoon dried thyme, or 4 sprigs fresh

1-1/2 pounds mixed mushrooms, quartered

1 bay leaf

1 10-ounce can diced tomatoes

1-1/2 cups Cabernet Franc

1-1/2 cups beef broth

1/2 teaspoon sugar

1 bunch chives, chopped

In a small bowl, mix the softened butter and flour and set it aside.

Over medium-high heat, brown the sausage in a large pan, crumbling it as it cooks. Remove the sausage from the pan, reduce the heat to medium, and add the olive oil, onion, celery, carrots, red pepper flakes and thyme. Cook until the vegetables begin to soften, approximately 5 minutes. Add the mushrooms and continue to cook until the mushrooms soften and begin to release some moisture. Scrape up the bits at the bottom of the pan with a wooden spoon.

Add the sausage back to the pan, add the bay leaf, tomatoes, wine and beef broth, and bring the mixture to a boil. Reduce the heat to medium-low. Cook the ragout for approximately 45 minutes, or until the liquid in the pan has reduced to about 1 cup. Add the sugar. If the sauce is still a little acidic, add a little bit more sugar, a 1/4 teaspoon at a time, tasting after each addition. Add the butter/flour mixture and stir until the sauce thickens. Season to taste with salt and pepper.

Serve the ragout over polenta and garnish with the chopped chives. Add a slice of crusty French bread to soak up the sauce.

CAROL SHELTON WINES

Greg Hallihan prepared this smoked filet for Winter WINEland in 2010, and it was such a hit that we had a ton of new visitors to the winery, who said they came because everyone was tweeting about our great smoky beef paired with our wines. In response, we convinced Greg to share this recipe and prepare the filet again, this time as sliders, for A Wine & Food Affair 2012.

3354-B Coffey Lane
Santa Rosa, CA
707-575-3441
carolshelton.com

FRENCH DIP SLIDERS
with karma au jus

chef Greg Hallihan

Pair with Carol Shelton Karma Zin

MAKES 48

1 small whole filet mignon,
2 to 4 pounds
8 tablespoons smoked sea
salt (if you do not have a
smoker)
½ bottle Carol Shelton
Karma Zin
32 ounces beef stock
6 ounces prepared raw
horseradish
12 ounces sour cream
48 slider or dinner rolls

If you have a smoker, prep it for cold smoking by placing a metal tray of ice just below the meat. This cools down the smoke and flavors the meat without cooking it. Use fruit wood chips for the cold smoke — apple or cherry wood are great, and grapevine prunings are even better. Do two smoking sessions of at least 45 minutes each.

If you do not have a smoker, rub the smoked sea salt well into the filet 1-2 days ahead of the day you want to cook it, so the salt and smoke work into the meat. After the rubbing or cold smoke has been done, grill or roast the meat as desired, preferably to rare-medium rare for the best flavor and texture. Slice the filet as thin as possible.

To prepare the Karma au jus, pour the Zinfandel into a saucepan and reduce the wine by half over medium heat. Add the beef stock and season with salt to taste.

To prepare the "Horsey Sauce," in a separate bowl, mix the horseradish and sour cream well with a whisk. Cover the bowl with plastic wrap and place it in the refrigerator until you're ready to serve the sliders.

To assemble the sliders, warm the buns on the grill and cut them in half. Spread the bottom bun slice with the horseradish sauce, add some sliced meat, and serve with a bowl of au jus for dipping.

CHATEAU DIANA

Sundays were always "Family Day," and every Sunday morning Mom would start cooking the sausages and meatballs, and simmer the sauce for hours in a huge pot — the same recipe our grandmother from Long Island prepared for years. Mom knew how to cook for a large family and made enough for leftovers. She always had a container in the freezer ready for any grandkids who came home from school hungry. The best part was making meatball or sausage sandwiches the next day.

6195 Dry Creek Road
Healdsburg CA 95448
707-433-6992
chateaud.com

mom's
SUNDAY SAUCE
with italian sausages & meatballs

chef Teri Manning

Pair with Chateau Diana 1221 Cabernet Sauvignon

SERVES 12

MEATBALLS
1 pound lean ground beef
½ pound Italian sausage, ground
1 egg
⅓ cup Italian bread crumbs
½ teaspoon black pepper
½ teaspoon fennel
2 teaspoons salt
½ small onion, finely chopped
3 cloves garlic, minced
2 tablespoons olive oil

SAUSAGE
3 mild Italian sausages
3 hot Italian sausages

SAUCE
4 28-ounce cans San Marzano stewed
   tomatoes (or equivalent fresh-stewed)
½ teaspoon red pepper flakes
2 teaspoons salt
1 teaspoon black pepper
1 bay leaf
2 tablespoons basil, finely chopped
3 cloves garlic, finely chopped
7 crimini mushrooms, chopped
½ cup 1221 Cabernet Sauvignon

POLENTA
1 quart water, plus more as needed
1 quart milk, plus more as needed
½ stick butter
2 tablespoons salt
4 cups polenta
1 cup creme fraiche
1 cup Parmigiano-Reggiano cheese, grated

To make the meatballs, combine all the ingredients except the olive oil in a large bowl. Roll the mixture into golf ball-size meatballs. Place the olive oil in a pot and heat it over medium-high heat. Add the meatballs one at a time and brown them on all sides, turning gently. Set the browned meatballs aside.

Place the sausages in the pan and brown them over medium-high heat, then set them aside.

To prepare the sauce, add all the ingredients to an 8-quart stockpot. Gently place the meatballs and sausages into the sauce and simmer on low for 2 to 3 hours.

While the sauce simmers, prepare the polenta. In a large, clean pot, bring the water, milk and butter to a boil. Add the salt and whisk in the polenta. Whisk constantly for 3 to 4 minutes to prevent lumps. Simmer the polenta for 45 minutes, partially covered and stirring every 10 minutes, until the polenta is thick. Add the creme fraiche and Parmesan. Add more milk if the polenta is too thick. Serve the sauce over the polenta.

D'ARGENZIO WINERY

This 1920s-era recipe is an Old World peasant dish our grandfather would make on Sundays for famiglia dinner. We carry on this Italian tradition on special occasions, including A Wine & Food Affair. Marinate the lamb one day in advance.

1301 Cleveland Avenue
Santa Rosa, CA 95401
707-280-4658
dargenziowine.com

SPIEDINI D' LOIODICE
con polenta enrico

chef Rosa di Loiodice

Pair with D'Argenzio Petite Sirah

SERVES 6

SPIEDINI

1 pound boneless leg of lamb, trimmed and cut into 1-inch cubes

2 tablespoons extra-virgin olive oil

sea salt and black pepper to taste

2 tablespoons fresh Italian parsley, chopped

1 tablespoon fresh mint, chopped

1 tablespoon fresh fennel, chopped

2 tablespoons wine vinegar

POLENTA

1 cup polenta

3-1/4 cups lukewarm water

1 teaspoon salt

1 tablespoon olive oil

1 to 2 tablespoons garlic powder (optional)

One day ahead, mix the cubed lamb in a bowl with the remaining spiedini ingredients. Cover the bowl with plastic wrap and place it in the refrigerator overnight, allowing the meat to marinate in the herbs.

Approximately 1 hour before you're ready to serve the spiedini, prepare the polenta.

Preheat the oven to 350°. Place all the polenta ingredients in a buttered 8-inch square pan.

Stir the mixture with a fork until the ingredients are blended, and bake the polenta uncovered for 50 minutes. Run a fork through it and bake for 10 more minutes.

While the polenta is baking, grill the lamb pieces for 6 to 8 minutes, or to your desired doneness. Let the meat rest for 5 minutes, and serve it with the cooked polenta.

DELOACH VINEYARDS

Pollo a la Catalana is a dish from the Catalonia region of Spain. Catalan cuisine is quite diverse, from the rich and savory stews cooked inland, to fish-based recipes along the coast. The cuisine includes many preparations that combine sweet with savory, including this one. It's great served over white rice.

1791 Olivet Road
Santa Rosa, CA 95401
707-526-9111
deloachvineyards.com

POLLO A LA CATALANA
(catalan-style chicken)

chef Sue Boy

Pair with DeLoach Russian River Valley Pinot Noir

SERVES 6

12 ounces pitted dried prunes

1 cup raisins

3-$^{1}/_{2}$ pounds boneless
  chicken thighs

olive oil

1 cup pine nuts

1-$^{1}/_{2}$ cups onions, chopped

3 ripe tomatoes, chopped

2 cups chicken broth

8 ounces light red wine
  (preferably Pinot Noir)

salt and pepper to taste

Place the prunes and raisins in a bowl, cover them with water, and allow them to soak for 4 hours.

Rinse the chicken thighs and pat them dry with paper towels. Season the chicken with salt and pepper. Add a few tablespoons of olive oil to a large frying pan and brown the chicken thighs. Remove the thighs from the pan and place them in a large open pot.

Drain the water from the soaked fruit and in the same pan used for browning the chicken, sauté the prunes, raisins and pine nuts. Add the chopped onions and continue to sauté, adding olive oil if necessary. Add the tomatoes and cook for approximately 5 minutes. Add the chicken broth and wine, and simmer the sauce for 10 minutes.

Pour the sauce over the chicken in the pot, bring the mixture to a simmer, and continue to simmer until the chicken is cooked through, about 30 minutes. Taste the sauce and adjust with salt and pepper, if needed. Serve the thighs and sauce over white rice.

DELORIMIER WINERY

I have said it before and I will say it again: BACON! It makes everything taste amazing. The full fruit flavor of the Primitivo wine complements the sour cherries in this dish, and the saltiness of the bacon adds a beautiful dimension to the wine. It's a perfect pairing! Marinate the pork shoulder two days before preparing this dish.

2001 Highway 128
Geyserville, CA 95448
707-857-2000
delorimierwinery.com

roasted

PORK SHOULDER

with dried cherry, bacon & sweet onion compote

chef Ryan Waldron

Pair with deLorimier Osborn Ranch Alexander Valley Primitivo

SERVES 6

PORK

3 pounds boneless pork shoulder

1 bottle dry red wine

grated zest and juice of ½ large
  orange

5 cloves garlic, crushed

12 fresh thyme sprigs

1 bay leaf

1 cinnamon stick

4-6 juniper berries, crushed

2 whole garlic cloves

kosher salt and freshly ground
  pepper

olive oil

COMPOTE

½ cup dried sour cherries

1-½ cups Primitivo or Zinfandel
  wine

⅓ pound bacon, cut into 1-inch
  pieces

12 ounces sweet onion, thinly
  sliced

2 bay leaves

2 tablespoons light molasses

¼ cup balsamic vinegar

kosher salt and freshly ground
  pepper

Two days before preparing this dish, place the pork shoulder in a container large enough for the meat and the marinade. Combine all the marinade ingredients (wine through the whole garlic cloves) in a bowl, mix well, and pour over the pork. Cover the container and place the pork in the refrigerator for 2 days, rotating it occasionally.

When it's time to cook the pork, preheat the oven to 500º. Remove the meat from the marinade and scrape everything off. Place the pork on a clean towel and dry the pork well. Rub it with a generous amount of salt and pepper.

Coat the bottom of a roasting pan with olive oil and place the pork in the pan, fat side up. Roast it in the oven for 30 minutes, reduce the temperature to 300º, and continue roasting until the internal temperature of the pork reaches 170º to 180º, about 2-1/2 to 3 hours. Remove the pan from the oven and tent the pork with foil. Let the meat stand for 15 minutes, shred or cut it to your liking, and set it aside.

To prepare the compote, combine the cherries and wine in a saucepan and bring the liquid to a slow simmer over medium heat. Remove the pan from the heat and let the mixture cool to room temperature. Then strain the cherries from the wine, retaining both.

Place the bacon in a large, heavy-bottom saucepan and cook it until it's crispy. Pour off the fat, except for 1/4 cup. Return the pan to medium heat with the 1/4 cup of fat and add the onions and bay leaves. Cook, stirring frequently, for 2 minutes. Reduce the heat to very low, cover the pan and cook, stirring occasionally, for about 18 minutes. Add the molasses and vinegar, raise the heat and bring the mixture to a boil. Add the cherry-infused wine and simmer the mixture for 10 minutes. Add the bacon and cherries, and season generously with salt and pepper. Serve the compote with the pork.

DUTTON ESTATE WINERY

This savory and spicy stew is a perfect pairing for our Karmen Isabella Pinot Noir, reflecting the bright cherry notes in the wine. Serve it over couscous made with chicken stock, lemon zest and chopped roasted pistachio nuts.

8757 Green Valley Road
Sebastopol, CA 95472
707-829-9463
duttonestatewinery.com

moroccan
LAMB STEW
with tart cherries

chef Cynthia Newcomb

Pair with Dutton Estate Karmen Isabella Pinot Noir

SERVES 6-8

1 tablespoon ground cumin

2 teaspoons ground coriander

1/2 teaspoon ground ginger

1/4 teaspoon ground cardamom

1/2 teaspoon fennel pollen or ground fennel

1/4 teaspoon chipotle powder or cayenne pepper

1/2 teaspoon ground black pepper

3 pounds trimmed and boned California leg of lamb or lamb shoulder, cut into 1-1/2-inch pieces

4 tablespoons olive oil

1 large onion, diced

1 tablespoon tomato paste

3 cloves garlic, minced

3 cups chicken broth

1 15-ounce can garbanzo beans, drained

1 15-ounce can chopped tomatoes

3 cinnamon sticks

2 tablespoons peeled fresh ginger, minced

2 teaspoons (packed) finely zested lemon peel

1 cup dried tart cherries

Mix the first 7 ingredients (cumin through black pepper) in a large bowl. Add the lamb pieces to the bowl and toss to coat the lamb. Heat 2 tablespoons of oil in a large, heavy-bottom skillet over medium-high heat. Working in batches, brown the meat on all sides, adding oil between batches. Transfer the lamb to another clean, large bowl after each batch.

Add the onion and tomato paste to the skillet, reduce the heat to medium, and sauté until the onions are soft. Add the garlic and cook 1 minute more. Add the broth and remaining ingredients, except the cherries. Bring the mixture to a boil, scraping up the browned bits from the bottom of the pan.

Add the lamb back to the skillet and bring the contents to a boil. Reduce the heat to low, partially cover the skillet and simmer for 1 hour. Add the cherries and continue simmering until the meat is tender, about 1/2 to 1 hour more. Serve warm.

You can prepare the lamb 1 day ahead. Allow it to cool, transfer it to a covered bowl and keep in the refrigerator. To serve, re-warm the lamb over low heat, stirring occasionally.

FRANCIS FORD COPPOLA'S WINERY

This recipe is taken from our Rustic menu and was inspired by a trip to Morocco: "If you ever visit the souk in Marrakesh, Morocco, you might come across a little man sitting on a big pile of rocks. If you order the lamb, he'll reach down and pull out a clay pot that has been covered in embers all night, inside of which is the most tender, falling-of-the-bone lamb you've ever had." We don't have a pile of rocks, so we cook our Marrakesh lamb in clay pots overnight in the oven and achieve the same results.

300 Via Archimedes
Geyserville, CA 95441
707-857-1485
franciscoppolawinery.com

rustic restaurant

MARRAKESH LAMB

recipe from Rustic: Francis's Favorites

Pair with Francis Ford Coppola Director's Cut Cinema

SERVES 6

½ cup turmeric
½ cup coriander
¼ cup ground fennel
¼ cup ground ginger
¼ cup cinnamon
½ cup kosher salt
2 tablespoons black pepper
6 pounds lamb shoulder
olive oil
juice of 2 lemons

Preheat oven to 225°.

In a large bowl, mix all the spices together and toss the raw lamb in the seasonings. Sear the lamb in olive oil on medium-high heat until it's golden brown.

Place the lamb in a heavy-bottom, oven-proof pan and add the lemon juice. Cover the meat with water and slow-cook it in the preheated oven for 8 to 9 hours, until the meat is tender.

Pour off the liquid in the pan and serve the lamb with your favorite grain. When Francis dines at Rustic, the Marrakesh lamb is served with couscous and a touch of harissa.

FRITZ WINERY

When it came time for us to select the perfect recipe for this year's event, we knew we couldn't do it without first choosing the perfect wine: our Estate Zinfandel. We put our heads together with Tracy Bidia of T & Company to create a dish that not only highlights the wine, but also warms the soul and pleases the taste buds on a cool fall day. Serve this dish with polenta, rice or wide noodles.

24691 Dutcher Creek Road
Cloverdale, CA 95425
707-894-3389
fritzwinery.com

ZIN-BRAISED BEEF

chef Tracy Bidia, T & Company

Pair with Fritz Estate Dry Creek Valley Zinfandel

SERVES 4-6

2 bottles Fritz Estate
   Zinfandel
2 tablespoons olive oil
3 pounds chuck, bottom
   round or top sirloin steak
salt and pepper
2 onions, peeled and cut into
   large dice
2 carrots, peeled and cut into
   large dice
2 stalks celery, cut into large
   dice
1 leek, white part only,
   cut into large dice
12 garlic cloves
2 sprigs fresh rosemary,
   leaves picked and finely
   chopped
6 sprigs thyme
2 quarts chicken stock

Preheat oven to 350°.

In a large saucepan, add the Zinfandel. Bring it to a boil, lower the heat, and let the wine simmer until it's reduced by 1/2. Set it aside.

Heat the olive oil in a large, heavy-bottom sauté or roasting pan. Season the beef generously with salt and pepper. Brown the beef on all sides, remove it from the pan and set it aside.

Remove all but 1 tablespoon of the oil from the pan. Add the vegetables, garlic, rosemary and thyme, and cook until they're lightly browned. Add the beef back to the pan, add the reduced wine, and cover with the chicken stock. Bring the contents to a simmer, cover the pan, and simmer for 2-1/2 to 3 hours, or until the meat is tender.

Place the beef on a platter. Strain the pan juices and bring them to a slight boil. Pour the juices over the beef and serve with any style of polenta, wide noodles or rice.

GEYSER PEAK WINERY

A grilled cheese sandwich might not be the first thing that comes to mind when you're contemplating what to enjoy with a glass of Geyser Peak Cabernet Sauvignon. But these sandwiches, filled with local St. George cheese, crispy bacon, caramelized onions and fresh herb aioli, nestled between grilled slices of sourdough, are the ideal choice!

22281 Chianti Road
Geyserville, CA 95441
707-857-9400
geyserpeakwinery.com

st. george & bacon
GRILLED CHEESE
with caramelized onions & herb aioli

chef Tim Vallery, Peloton Catering

Pair with Geyser Peak Cabernet Sauvignon

MAKES 4 SANDWICHES

ONIONS
1 ounce olive oil
2 sweet yellow onions, sliced
1 ounce Geyser Peak Cabernet
   Sauvignon

AIOLI
1/4 cup garlic, poached
2 egg yolks
1/4 cup extra-virgin olive oil
3/4 cup canola oil
1/2 lemon, zest and juice
1/2 teaspoon fresh thyme,
   chopped
1/2 teaspoon Italian parsley,
   chopped
kosher salt
fresh ground black pepper

SANDWICHES
unsalted butter, softened, as
   needed
8 slices sourdough bread
8 slices Matos St. George cheese
8 slices bacon, cooked
1/4 cup caramelized onions
4 tablespoons herb aioli

To prepare the caramelized onions, heat a stainless steel pan on low to medium heat, add the olive oil, and then the onions. Sweat the onions for 1 hour. Deglaze the onions with the wine and continue to sweat the onions until they are well caramelized. Let them cool.

To prepare the aioli, place the garlic and egg yolks in a food processor and puree them. Slowly drizzle in the olive and canola oils, keeping the mixture emulsified. Add the lemon zest, lemon juice and herbs, and season with salt and pepper. Chill the mixture before you're ready to use it.

To prepare the sandwiches, spread butter on both sides of the bread slices. Layer the ingredients on one side of the bread and top with the other. In a panini press, cook the sandwiches until the cheese is melted in the center, and serve.

GRATON RIDGE CELLARS

When pondering a recipe for this year, we asked ourselves," What goes with Pinot Noir?" The best answer came to us around springtime: lamb! Then the question was how to make it in a form that everyone can easily enjoy. Meatballs, of course! And of course, you cover anything in a mushroom sauce, and bam! The perfect food to pair with our Russian River Pinot Noir.

3561 Gravenstein Highway North
Sebastopol, CA 95472
707-823-3040
gratonridge.com

sicilian
LAMB MEATBALLS

chef Gerard Guidice, Sally Tomatoes

Pair with Graton Ridge Russian River Valley Pinot Noir

SERVES 6-8

MEATBALLS

1 pound ground lamb

1 cup toasted French bread crumbs

½ cup Parmesan cheese

¼ cup chopped Italian parsley

2 garlic cloves, minced

½ cup cream

1 teaspoon kosher salt

½ teaspoon pepper

SAUCE

¼ cup extra-virgin olive oil

2 teaspoons garlic, slivered

5 cups chopped Roma tomatoes, well drained

2 portobello mushrooms, gills removed and cut into ½-inch pieces

½ cup dry Marsala wine

½ cup fresh basil, chopped

1 teaspoon crushed red pepper flakes

To prepare the meatballs, combine all the ingredients in a large bowl. Roll the mixture into golf ball-size rounds and gently sauté them in a non-stick skillet coated with olive oil, until the meatballs are cooked to 160° and with a light pink center.

To prepare the sauce, heat the olive oil in a sauté pan over medium heat and add the garlic, cooking it until it's light brown. Add the chopped tomatoes and mushrooms and cook over high heat for 3 minutes. Add the Marsala and continue to cook until the alcohol has burned off. Add the basil and pepper flakes, reduce the heat to a simmer, and allow the mixture to reduce for 5 minutes.

Add the meatballs to the sauce and simmer 5 to 10 minutes more. Serve the meatballs over rigatoni topped with shaved ricotta salata cheese.

HOOK AND LADDER WINERY

Osso Buco has been a favorite of mine for as long as I can remember. Then a number of years ago I decided not to eat veal, and there went my Osso Buco. Unable to cope with the loss of my all-time favorite dish, I experimented with beef shanks in place of the traditional veal shanks. This adaptation has worked well, and once again the luscious smells and taste of Osso Buco fill my kitchen and my dining table.

2134 Olivet Road
Santa Rosa, CA 95401
707-526-2255
hookandladderwinery.com

not so traditional

OSSO BUCO

with gremolata

chef Christine DeLoach

Pair with Hook & Ladder Merlot

SERVES 4

OSSO BUCO

4 beef shanks, cut into 2-inch-thick slices

1-1/2 cups plus 3 tablespoons flour

1 teaspoon salt

1 teaspoon pepper

2 tablespoons butter

2 tablespoons olive oil

1 medium onion, finely chopped

2 medium carrots, finely chopped

1-1/2 stalks celery, finely chopped

2 cloves garlic, very finely minced

3-4 sprigs fresh thyme

1-1/2 cups dry white wine

2-3 cups Roma tomatoes, peeled and coarsely chopped (or canned with their juice)

1-1/2 cups chicken stock

3/4 teaspoon salt

1 teaspoon pepper

3 tablespoons flour

GREMOLATA

4 large garlic cloves, very finely minced

1/2 cup lemon zest

3/4 cup Italian parsley, chopped

Preheat oven to 325°

In a large bowl, dredge the shanks in 1-1/2 cups flour that has been seasoned with the salt and pepper. In a Dutch oven, melt the butter and olive oil over moderate heat. Add the shank pieces and cook 5-6 minutes until they're browned on all sides. Remove the meat from the pot.

To the same pot, add a little olive oil if necessary and sauté the onion, carrots and celery for 6-7 minutes. Add the garlic and thyme, and cook another 5 minutes. Add the browned shanks to the vegetables, and turn the heat to low. Add the wine and simmer for 5 minutes, then add the tomatoes, stock, salt and pepper. Stir gently to blend.

Place the pot in the preheated oven and cook the beef for 2 hours. Remove the pot from the oven and stir in the flour to thicken the liquid. (To avoid lumping, whisk the flour and some of the liquid in a separate bowl before adding it to the pot.) Return the pot to the oven for an additional 30 minutes.

While the shanks cook, prepare the gremolata by combining the garlic, lemon zest and parsley in a small bowl. The shanks should be very tender when done. Just prior to serving, add the gremolata. Place the osso buco on a warmed serving platter and serve with polenta or egg noodles.

HUDSON STREET WINERIES

I developed the basic recipe a few years ago and discovered how well it went with Zinfandel. Because I like to play with my food, I kept working on the barbecue sauce and eventually came up with this Asian version, which adds layers and depth of flavor that match nicely with the spice in the Shippey Zinfandel. Be sure to marinate the ribs in the dry rub overnight.

428 Hudson Street
Healdsburg CA 95448
707-433-2364
hudsonstreetwineries.com

lip smackin'
BABY BACK RIBS

chef Jeff Young, J. Young Culinary/TWIST – an eatery

Pair with Shippey Vineyards Rocking Z Vineyard Zinfandel

SERVES 2-3

DRY RUB

⅓ cup brown sugar
2 tablespoons chili powder
1 tablespoon kosher salt
1 rack baby back ribs

BASTING SAUCE

½ cup soy sauce
2 tablespoons sesame oil
6 cloves garlic, minced
1 cup water
2 tablespoons oyster sauce
1 tablespoon Thai red curry
    paste
¼ cup honey
¼ cup molasses

To prepare the dry rub for the ribs, mix the first three ingredients together in a small bowl. Place the ribs on a sheet pan and coat them with the spice mixture. Cover the ribs and refrigerate them overnight.

Before grilling the meat, combine all the basting sauce ingredients in a saucepan and simmer the mixture on medium heat for 5 minutes or until thoroughly blended. Grill the ribs over indirect heat for 1-1/2 to 2 hours or until tender, basting with the sauce every 10 to 15 minutes.

J. RICKARDS WINERY

This recipe appeared in the Silver Palate Cookbook three decades ago, and since then, Oprah, Woman's Day magazine and many others have raved about its complex flavors and simplicity. We've put our own spin on it by adding citrus and red wine. Any of our Zinfandels can be used, and pair beautifully with the finished dish. We especially like it with our Ancestor Selections Zinfandel, a classic example of the field-blend style of Zin. Marinate the chicken overnight before continuing with the recipe.

24505 Chianti Road
Cloverdale, CA 95425
707-758-3441
jrwinery.com

CHICKEN MARBELLA

chef Dan Lucia, DL Catering; recipe by Eliza Rickards

Pair with J. Rickards Ancestor Selections Zinfandel

SERVES 4-6

1/2 cup J. Rickards Zinfandel

1/4 cup extra-virgin olive oil

1/4 cup red wine vinegar

1/2 cup raisins

1/2 cup pitted Kalamata olives, halved

1/4 cup drained capers, plus 1 tablespoon packing liquid

1/2 orange, unpeeled, quartered and cut into 1/4-inch slices

1/2 lemon, unpeeled, quartered and cut into 1/4-inch slices

4 bay leaves

6 cloves garlic, thinly sliced

2 tablespoons fresh rosemary, chopped

2 teaspoons kosher salt

1 teaspoon freshly ground black pepper

3-1/2 to 4 pounds chicken thighs, legs, breasts

1/4 cup packed light brown sugar

One day ahead, combine the wine, olive oil, vinegar, raisins, olives, capers and their liquid, orange, lemon, bay leaves, garlic, rosemary, salt and pepper in a large bowl. Place the chicken pieces in a large resealable bag and add the wine mixture. Seal the bag, squeezing out as much air as possible. Refrigerate the chicken for 12 to 24 hours, turning the bag occasionally.

When you're ready to prepare the dish, preheat the oven to 350°. Arrange the chicken, skin side up, in a single layer on a large rimmed baking sheet. Squeeze the marinade mixture, including the fruit, olives and capers, out of the bag and over the chicken. Sprinkle the brown sugar on top and bake, basting every 15 or 20 minutes, until the chicken is cooked through, 50 to 60 minutes total.

To serve, transfer the chicken, olives, fruit and capers to a serving dish, using a slotted spoon. Spoon the pan juices over the top of the chicken — you can skim off the fat and reduce the juices a bit in a saucepan, if you'd like. This dish can be served hot or at room temperature.

KACHINA VINEYARDS

We like to experiment with different cultural foods to see how they pair with our wines. We find that the more exotic foods have very distinct flavor profiles and complement our big, bold wines surprisingly well.

4551 Dry Creek Road
Healdsburg, CA 95448
707-332-7917
kachinavineyards.com

CUBAN PORK STEW
with sweet potato mash

chef Mike Matson, Vintage Valley Catering

Pair with Kachina Vineyards Cabernet Sauvignon

SERVES 8

1/2 pound smoked bacon,
   cut into small dice
3 pounds pork shoulder,
   cut into 1-inch cubes
salt and pepper
1 tablespoon cumin
1-1/2 cups red bell pepper,
   cut into medium dice
1-1/2 cups red onion, cut into
   medium dice
4 garlic cloves, chopped
2 cups Kachina Cabernet
   Sauvignon
1/3 cup orange juice
2 tablespoons lime juice
2 quarts chicken stock
4 cups tomatoes, diced
2 tablespoons tomato paste
3 pounds sweet potato, cubed
1/2 cup butter
1/3 cup green onions, chopped
2 tablespoons parsley,
   chopped

In a medium-size soup pot, brown the bacon and set it aside. Leave the bacon grease in the pot on medium heat.

Season the pork shoulder with salt, pepper and cumin. Sear the shoulder until it's golden brown. Set it aside with the bacon.

Sauté the peppers, red onions and garlic in the pot. Add the pork, Cabernet Sauvignon, orange and lime juice and reduce the mixture slightly. Add the chicken stock, tomatoes and tomato paste. Bring the pot to a boil and simmer the mixture until the pork is tender.

Preheat the oven to 375° and roast the sweet potatoes until they're soft. Let them cool slightly, then peel the potatoes and roughly mash them with the butter.

To serve, place a large spoonful of mashed sweet potato on each plate and top generously with the pork stew. Garnish with the chopped green onions and parsley.

KENDALL-JACKSON HEALDSBURG

The rich flavor of braised short ribs pairs wonderfully with the balanced tannins in the Jackson Hills Cabernet Sauvignon. We like to serve this with truffled celery root puree; the freshness of the celery root and the earthiness of the black truffles complements this lush and elegant wine.

337 Healdsburg Avenue
Healdsburg, CA 95448
707-433-7102
kj.com

red wine-braised
SHORT RIBS
with truffled celery root puree

Recipe by Kendall-Jackson Culinary Team

Pair with Kendall-Jackson Jackson Hills Cabernet Sauvignon

SERVES 4

SHORT RIBS

5 pounds beef short ribs (bone in)
kosher salt
freshly ground black pepper
$\frac{1}{4}$ cup rice oil
2 carrots, large dice
2 celery, large dice
1 onion, large dice
2 slices bacon, minced
2 tablespoons tomato paste
3 cups red wine, such as
  Cabernet Sauvignon
2 quarts veal stock (or low-sodium
  beef stock)
1 sachet containing 1 sprig thyme,
1 tablespoon black peppercorns,
1 tablespoon allspice and 1 bay leaf

PUREE

1-$\frac{1}{2}$ pounds celery root, peeled and
  cut into $\frac{1}{2}$-inch pieces
$\frac{1}{2}$ cup russet potatoes, peeled and
  cut into $\frac{1}{2}$-inch pieces
1 cup heavy cream
kosher salt
freshly ground black pepper
$\frac{1}{2}$ cup truffle butter ($\frac{1}{2}$ cup unsalted
  butter with 1 tablespoon truffle oil
  can be substituted)

Remove the short ribs from the refrigerator and bring them to room temperature. Season the ribs liberally with salt and pepper.

Preheat the oven to 300°.

Heat a large sauté pan until it's almost smoking. Add the rice oil and brown the ribs on all sides until they are very dark, but not burnt. Remove the meat from the pan and place it in a roasting pan.

In the same sauté pan, cook the vegetables until they're golden brown. Add the bacon and cook 1 minute more. Add the tomato paste and stir until all the vegetables are coated and nicely caramelized. Deglaze the pan with the wine and reduce by 80%. Add the vegetable mixture to the roasting pan holding the ribs, followed by the veal stock. Place the roasting pan over medium-high heat and bring the contents to a simmer. Skim off any foam that comes to the surface. Add the spice sachet and tightly cover the roasting pan with foil. Braise the ribs in the oven until they're fork tender, approximately 3 hours.

Remove the ribs from the oven and let them cool in the braising liquid. When they are cool enough to handle, remove the ribs from the braising liquid and discard any excess fat, gristle and bone. Skim off any fat from the liquid and strain out all the vegetables. Return the liquid to a simmer and reduce by half. Strain the braising liquid through a fine sieve and pour over the short ribs.

To prepare the celery root puree, place the celery root, potatoes and cream in a heavy-bottomed pot. Bring to a simmer, season with salt, and cover the pot. Cook, covered, for approximately 6 to 8 minutes, or until the potatoes and celery root are tender. Remove the pot from the heat and strain the liquid from the solids, reserving the cream. Place the potato and celery root in a blender and add half of the liquid. Puree and add only as much liquid as is needed. Season to taste with salt and pepper, then blend in the butter. Serve the puree warm, or chill it and reheat with leftover cream.

KENDALL-JACKSON WINE CENTER

The quality of American Wagyu beef, often called American Kobe beef, is amazing and makes the best trip-tip, to our minds. The richness of the Kobe pairs wonderfully with the tangy Cabernet-braised red cabbage and blue cheese in these sandwiches.

5007 Fulton Road
Fulton, CA 95439
707-571-8100
kj.com

kobe
TRI-TIP SANDWICHES
with cabernet-braised cabbage & blue cheese-buttermilk dressing

recipe by Kendall-Jackson Culinary Team

Pair with Kendall-Jackson Hawkeye Mountain Cabernet Sauvignon

SERVES 6

DRESSING
1 pound crumbled blue cheese
1 cup mayonnaise
$^1/_2$ cup sour cream
2 cups buttermilk
2 teaspoons garlic, chopped
$^1/_4$ cup chives, minced
$^1/_2$ cup scallions (including green part),
    minced
$^1/_4$ cup shallots, minced
2 teaspoons kosher salt
1 teaspoon freshly ground black pepper

TRI-TIP
2-$^1/_2$ - to 3-pound tri-tip
1 tablespoon olive oil
2 tablespoons kosher salt
1 tablespoon freshly ground
    black pepper

CABBAGE
1 tablespoon bacon fat or olive oil
$^1/_2$ red onion, julienned
$^1/_2$ tablespoon kosher salt
1 pound red cabbage, thinly sliced
1 sachet containing 1 bay leaf, 4 juniper
    berries, 3 black peppercorns
$^1/_3$ cup red wine vinegar
1 cup red wine, such as
    Cabernet Sauvignon
$^1/_8$ cup pomegranate molasses
$^1/_8$ cup sugar
1 sprig fresh rosemary

Prepare the dressing one day ahead by combining all ingredients in a mixing bowl. Cover the bowl with plastic wrap and refrigerate overnight.

To prepare the tri-tip, remove it from the refrigerator and allow it to sit at room temperature for 1 hour. Preheat a grill to high heat. Pat the tri-tip dry with paper towels. Rub the tri-tip with olive oil and season with salt and pepper. Place the meat on the grill for 4 minutes, flip it over and cook the other side for 4 minutes more.

Move the tri-tip to a medium-low-heat area on your grill and cook it for another 20 to 25 minutes, or until the internal temperature reaches 134°. Remove the beef from the grill, loosely tent it with foil and allow it to rest for 15 minutes before slicing the tri-tip against the grain.

To prepare the cabbage, in a large pot over medium heat, add the bacon fat, onion and salt. Sauté until the onions are soft, without letting them brown, for approximately 4 minutes, stirring occasionally. Add the cabbage and sachet to the pot, stir, and wilt the cabbage slightly, approximately 4 minutes. Add the red wine vinegar, wine, pomegranate molasses, sugar and rosemary sprig. Stir and bring to a boil. Reduce the heat to a simmer and cook the cabbage for approximately 30 minutes, or until the liquid reduces almost completely. Discard the sachet and rosemary sprig.

To assemble the sandwiches, toast or grill some hearty bread, such as ciabatta. Spoon the cabbage on the bottom slice of bread, layer with some tri-tip and top with the blue cheese dressing and remaining slice of bread.

KOKOMO WINERY

In Italian, "osso" means "bone" and "buco" means "hole." Part of what makes osso buco so delicious is that the slow cooking process coaxes all that sublime bone marrow flavor from the "hole of the bone." This dish is a home favorite, as it fills the air with savory aromas while the pork cooks. Serve it with a loaf of hot, crusty bread and our hearty Malbec.

4791 Dry Creek Road
Healdsburg, CA 95448
707-433-0200
kokomowines.com

OSSO BUCO STEW
with gremolata & freeze-dried corn

chef Jason Denton, Jackson's Bar & Oven

Pair with Kokomo Malbec

SERVES 4

1 sprig fresh rosemary

1 sprig fresh thyme

1 bay leaf

2 whole cloves

3 whole pork shanks
   (about 1 pound per shank)

sea salt

freshly ground black pepper

all-purpose flour, for dredging

½ cup vegetable oil

1 small onion, ½-inch dice

1 small carrot, ½-inch dice

1 stalk celery, ½-inch dice

2 tablespoons tomato paste

1 cup Kokomo Malbec

3 cups chicken stock

3 tablespoons flat-leaf Italian
   parsley, chopped

1 tablespoon lemon zest

3 cloves garlic, chopped

3 tablespoons olive oil

2 tablespoons freeze-dried
   corn

Place the rosemary, thyme, bay leaf and cloves on a 6-inch square of cheesecloth and tie the bouquet garni tightly with kitchen twine.

Pat the pork shanks dry with paper towels and season them with salt and pepper. Dredge the shanks in the flour, shaking off the excess.

In a large Dutch oven, heat the vegetable oil until it starts to smoke. Add the pork shanks to the pan and brown them on all sides, about 3 minutes per side. Remove the browned shanks and set them aside.

In the same pot, add the onion, carrot and celery. Season with salt and sauté the vegetables until they're soft and translucent, about 8 minutes. Add the tomato paste and mix well. Return the browned shanks to the pan, add the wine, and reduce the liquid by half, about 5 minutes. Add the bouquet garni and 2 cups of the chicken stock and bring the mixture to a boil. Reduce the heat to low, cover the pan and simmer the mixture for approximately 1-1/2 hours, or until the meat falls off the bone. Check every 15 minutes, turning the shanks and adding more chicken stock as necessary; the level of cooking liquid should always be 3/4 the way up the shanks.

When the pork is done, remove and discard the bouquet garni from the pot. Remove the shanks and pull the meat off the bone. Add the meat back to the pot.

Quickly prepare the gremolata by combining the chopped parsley, lemon zest, chopped garlic and olive oil. To serve, ladle the stew into bowls and garnish with the gremolata and freeze-dried corn.

KRUTZ FAMILY CELLARS

One of the great things about cooking is the fusion of different cultural tastes into something new. This recipe melds our Southern heritage with our current wine country lifestyle. The sausage is for all the fall Saturdays spent watching Southeastern Conference football games, and the Syrah sauce is for all the days we spend with the vines. It's a perfect game-day snack.

1301 Cleveland Avenue, Suite B
Santa Rosa, CA 95401
707-536-1532
krutzfamilycellars.com

SAUSAGE SKEWERS

with mushrooms & syrah dipping sauce

recipe by Krutz staff; sauce by Dylan Sheldon

Pair with Krutz Family Cellars Syrah

SERVES 5-7

DIPPING SAUCE

olive oil, for coating the pan

¼ cup shallots, minced

¼ cup fennel, minced

½ cup Krutz Syrah

½ cup beef stock

2 tablespoons unsalted butter

1 tablespoon fresh thyme, finely chopped

kosher salt and freshly ground black pepper to taste

SKEWERS

16 to 20 small crimini mushrooms

1 tablespoon olive oil

salt and pepper to taste

1 pound sausage links (your favorite)

toothpicks

To prepare the dipping sauce, heat a sauté pan over medium-high heat and add enough olive oil to coat the pan. Add the shallots and fennel and cook until they're translucent.

Place the cooked shallots and fennel in a blender, add the Syrah, and puree until the mixture is smooth. Return the mixture to the pan and cook until the liquid is reduced by half. Add the beef stock, butter and thyme, and sauté for 3 minutes on low heat. Season with salt and pepper, and set the sauce aside while you assemble and cook the sausage skewers.

Prepare a grill for direct-heat cooking.

Wipe the mushrooms clean with a towel and place them in a small bowl. Add the olive oil, salt and pepper, and mix well. Over low heat, grill the whole mushrooms until they're tender, being careful not to let them fall through the grate. Grill the sausages according to directions on the package, and cut them into 1-inch pieces.

To serve, thread 1 sausage piece on a toothpick, and then a mushroom. Dip in the reduction sauce and enjoy.

LA CREMA WINERY

Coq au vin is a classic French peasant dish traditionally prepared with rooster. In this version, we use chicken legs, which are not only easier to find, but also require a fraction of the cooking time. This is a great dish for a cold winter's night, and while the recipe must be started one day ahead, the end result is well worth the effort.

235 Healdsburg Avenue
Healdsburg, CA 95448
707-431-9400
lacrema.com

COQ AU VIN
(chicken with wine)

chef Eric Frischkorn

Pair with La Crema Russian River Valley Pinot Noir

SERVES 8

8 chicken legs
kosher salt
freshly ground black pepper
2 tablespoons oil
2 yellow onions, large dice
3 celery stalks, large dice
2 carrots, large dice
5 garlic cloves, crushed
1 bottle La Crema Russian River Valley Pinot Noir
1 bunch thyme, plus a few sprigs picked, chopped and reserved for garnish
10 black peppercorns
½ bunch parsley, leaves chopped fine and stems reserved
2 bay leaves
4 cups chicken stock
6 ounces slab bacon, medium dice
8 ounces small button mushrooms
8 ounces pearl onions
¼ cup all-purpose flour

Season the chicken with salt and pepper. Heat the oil in a large sauté pan over medium-high heat. Add the chicken and sear the legs until they're golden brown, but not cooked through. Remove the chicken and add the onion, celery, carrot and garlic to the pan; cook until they begin to caramelize. Deglaze the pan with 1/4 cup of the wine.

Prepare a sachet by wrapping the thyme sprigs, peppercorns, parsley stems and bay leaves in a 6-inch square of cheesecloth. Tie up the packet with kitchen twine. In a plastic container, add the chicken, vegetables, sachet and the remaining wine. Allow the contents to cool and then refrigerate for 12 to 24 hours.

The following day, preheat the oven to 300°.

Strain the chicken and vegetables, reserving the wine and sachet. Place the wine in a braising pan and reduce the liquid to 1 cup over medium heat. Add the chicken stock, chicken, vegetables and sachet, and bring to a light simmer. Cover the pan and place it in the oven for 1 hour, or until the chicken is tender.

Meanwhile, in a 6-quart pot, cook the bacon over medium heat. Once the fat has rendered, add the mushrooms and onions. Cook for 5 minutes. Add the flour and stir the roux until it begins to brown lightly.

Remove the braising pan from the oven and transfer the chicken to a warm plate. Strain the braising liquid through a sieve and discard the sachet and vegetables. Pour the liquid into the pot with the roux and whisk rapidly. Bring the liquid to a boil and reduce to a simmer, skimming any solids that rise to the surface.

To serve, season the coq au vin with salt, pepper and some of the remaining chopped herbs. Place the chicken over egg noodles or mashed potatoes, with a heaping ladle of sauce.

LIMERICK LANE CELLARS

Jake and Alexis Bilbro took over Limerick Lane in 2011. As new owners, they bring new ideas and prior experiences to the winery. One of the best new things they brought was this recipe from Jake's father's family. These sausages are flavorful and spiced right for pairing with red wine.

1023 Limerick Lane
Healdsburg, CA 95448
707-433-9211
limericklanewines.com

WILD BOAR SAUSAGE

chefs Peter Leary and Jake Bilbro

Pair with Limerick Lane Estate Grown Zinfandel

MAKES 3 POUNDS
1 clove garlic, peeled
1 cup white wine
1-$\frac{1}{2}$ pounds ground wild boar
1-$\frac{1}{2}$ pounds ground pork
4 teaspoons salt
2 teaspoons pepper
1 teaspoon nutmeg
1 teaspoon allspice

Place the garlic and white wine in a food processor and process them into a paste. Let the paste stand at room temperature for at least 1 hour.

Combine the boar and pork in a bowl and spread the mixture out on a clean work surface. Wrap the garlic-wine paste in a porous cloth (we use a clean T-shirt) and squeeze the garlic-infused wine over the ground meat. Sprinkle the salt, pepper, nutmeg and allspice over the meat and mix it all together. At this point, you can leave the sausage in bulk or stuff it into casings.

Grill the patties or links for 6 to 10 minutes per side, and serve them on rolls with mustard.

LOCALS TASTING ROOM

My nonno secondo, Valentino Bugica, would make this ragu every Sunday with his brother, Primo. One would always argue with the other about whether sausage should be included or not. Some Sundays, Primo would win; some Sundays, Valentino would win. You decide whether you want sausage in the sauce or not.

21023-A Geyserville Avenue
Geyserville, CA 95441
707-857-4900
tastelocalwines.com

OXTAIL & SHORT RIB RAGU
over soft polenta

chef Dino Bugica, Diavola Pizzeria

Pair with Praxis Lagrein

SERVES 4

2 pounds oxtail

3 pounds short ribs

2 tablespoons olive oil

2 large onions, thickly sliced

4 stalks of celery, thickly sliced

3 large carrots, thickly sliced

6 garlic cloves

1-$\frac{1}{2}$ cups dry red wine

2 tablespoons tomato paste

2 bay leaves

2 cups veal or chicken stock

kosher salt

black pepper

POLENTA

1 gallon milk

sage to taste

3 cups polenta

salt and pepper to taste

1 pound butter

Preheat oven to 300°.

Season the oxtail and short rib meat with salt and pepper. In a heavy-bottom pan, heat the olive oil over medium-high heat. In batches, brown the meat in the pan, then transfer the pieces to a plate.

Discard the fat from the meat and place the meat into a pot. Add the onion, celery, carrot and garlic cloves, then add the red wine. Add the tomato paste, bay leaves and stock, cover the pot with parchment paper and then a lid. Cook for 3 to 4 hours, or until the meat is tender.

Remove the meat from the pot and remove the bone. Return the meat to the pot and skim off the fat. Keep the meat warm.

To prepare the polenta, bring the milk and sage to a boil in a large saucepan, then slowly add the polenta, salt and pepper, mixing constantly. Turn the heat to low, add the butter, cover the pot and cook the polenta for 30 minutes, or until it's tender.

Serve the braised meat over the polenta.

LONGBOARD VINEYARDS

Syrah is sexy, and so is this recipe. The lusciousness of chocolate, the spicy bite of chiles and the comforting richness of bacon got us all hot and bothered when Jude Affronti let us taste this delicious dish at our Surf Lounge.

5 Fitch Street
Healdsburg, CA 95448
707-433-3473
longboardvineyards.com

SOUL SURFER RIBS

chef Jude Affronti

Pair with Longboard Vineyards Russian River Valley Syrah

SERVES 6-8

6 ounces thick-sliced bacon
salt and pepper to taste
4 pounds boneless short ribs
flour, for dredging
½ cup shallots, chopped
½ cup pasilla chiles, chopped
3 garlic cloves, minced
2 cups Longboard Syrah
4 cups stock
1 cup tomatoes, peeled,
   chopped and drained
1 sprig thyme
1 bay leaf
3 tablespoons bittersweet
   chocolate, shaved or grated
½ teaspoon unsweetened
   cocoa powder (preferably
   Dutch-process)

In a large, heavy-bottomed pot over medium heat, render the bacon until it's crisp. Using a slotted spoon, transfer the bacon to paper towels to drain.

While the bacon cooks, season the ribs with salt and pepper, then dredge them in flour, patting off any excess. Working in batches, brown the ribs in the bacon drippings in a pot over medium-high heat, until the ribs are brown on all sides, about 8 minutes per batch. Transfer them to a plate.

Add the shallots, chilies and garlic to the pot. Reduce the heat to medium and cook until the vegetables are soft, stirring occasionally, about 10 minutes.

Add the wine, increase the heat to high, and boil until the liquid is reduced by half, scraping up the browned bits (about 5 minutes). Add the stock, tomatoes, thyme, bay leaf and cooked bacon. Return the ribs to the pot, cover and reduce the heat to medium-low. Simmer the ribs for 90 minutes. Uncover the pot and continue to simmer the ribs until the meat is tender, stirring occasionally, about 90 minutes longer.

Transfer the ribs to a plate, cover them loosely with foil, and keep in a warm place. Remove the bay leaf and thyme sprig from the pot, and skim the fat from the surface of the sauce. Increase the heat to medium-high and reduce the sauce until it begins to thicken, about 8 minutes. Reduce the heat to medium, add the chocolate and cocoa powder, and stir until the chocolate melts. Season to taste with salt and pepper. Return the ribs to the pot, turning to coat them in sauce, and simmer briefly to re-warm, about 5 minutes. Serve the ribs with mashed parsnips or potatoes.

LOST CANYON WINERY

Our caterer, Kris Graves, is a local firefighter who works in Lodi. Last year Kris and his twin brother, Michael, won the Food Network's 24 Hour Restaurant Battle. Kris' pork tenderloin with cranberry chutney is one of his favorite things to make at the firehouse, and he likes to serve it with roasted potatoes and grilled veggies. We decided to change up the recipe a bit and serve the pork open-faced on a Hawaiian sweet roll.

123 4th Street
Santa Rosa, CA 95401
707-623-9621
lostcanyonwinery.com

IT'S JUST PORK...
& chutney

chef Kris Graves

Pair with Lost Canyon Morelli Lane Vineyard Russian River Valley Pinot Noir

SERVES 4-6

PORK
1 teaspoon ground cinnamon
1 teaspoon cumin
1 teaspoon chili powder
1 teaspoon paprika
1 teaspoon fennel seed
1 teaspoon salt
1 teaspoon black pepper
1 pork tenderloin
1 tablespoon olive oil
3 Hawaiian bread rolls,
   cut in half

CHUTNEY
1 onion, finely chopped
6 to 8 cloves garlic, minced
¼ teaspoon ground cloves
2 tablespoons ground ginger
¼ cup red wine vinegar
¼ cup granulated sugar
½ cup water
salt and pepper to taste
6 ounces dried cranberries

To prepare the pork, preheat the oven to 350°. Mix all the dry ingredients together and coat the pork generously with the rub. Let the loin rest for 1 hour to let the seasonings set in.

Place the oil in a hot skillet and sear the pork on all sides, roughly 4 to 5 minutes. Place the pork in a baking dish and bake it in the oven until it reaches your desired degree of doneness, about 25 to 30 minutes, depending on the size of the loin.

While the pork is in the oven, place all the chutney ingredients except for the dried cranberries into a medium saucepan. Bring the mixture to a boil. Add the cranberries, reduce the heat and simmer until the cranberries have rehydrated. If the liquid evaporates before the cranberries soften, just add more water and keep cooking until you achieve the desired consistency. The chutney should be on the firm, chunky side of a jelly.

When the pork is done, remove it from the oven and let it rest for at least 10 minutes. Slice the meat into 1-inch-thick pieces. Place 1 slice of meat on each half of the Hawaiian sweet rolls, spoon a generous portion of the chutney over the pork, and serve.

LYNMAR ESTATE

Wine and food pairings are our passion, and chef David Frakes' inspiration for them comes from our organic culinary gardens. With its warm and spicy aromas, there's nothing better than a steamy bowl of savory chili paired with our Russian River Valley Pinot Noir to warm you up on a cold winter evening.

3909 Frei Road
Sebastopol, CA 95472
707-829-3374
lynmarestate.com

turkey & white bean
CHILI

chef David Frakes

Pair with Lynmar Estate Russian River Valley Pinot Noir

SERVES 8-10

6 slices thick-cut applewood-smoked bacon, cut into 1/2-inch pieces
4 cloves garlic, finely minced
2 medium yellow onions, finely chopped
1 large red bell pepper, seeded and chopped into 1/4-inch dice
1 large yellow pepper, seeded and chopped into 1/4-inch dice
3 tablespoons chili powder
1 tablespoon ancho chili powder
1 tablespoon cumin, toasted and ground
2 teaspoons oregano
1 tablespoon paprika (smoked or regular)
salt and freshly cracked black pepper to taste
1 pound lean (85%) ground beef
1 pound ground turkey
1 cup dark Mexican beer
1 15-ounce can white beans, drained and rinsed
1 24-ounce can crushed tomatoes
1 24-ounce can diced tomatoes, with juice

GARNISHES
lime wedges
sour cream
shredded Cheddar cheese, preferably sharp and local
scallions, sliced super-fine on bias

In a large heavy-bottomed Dutch oven, cook the bacon over medium heat until the pieces are lightly crisp, stirring occasionally. Add the garlic, onions, bell peppers, chili powders, cumin, oregano and paprika, and season with salt and pepper. Cook the mixture until the vegetables are tender and the seasonings are aromatic.

Add the beef and break it up with a wooden spoon. Once the beef is broken up and beginning to brown, add the ground turkey. Break it up with the spoon and brown it until it's no longer pink, roughly 4 minutes. Stir in the beer and beans. Add the crushed and diced tomatoes. Turn the heat down to low and simmer for 1-1/2 to 2 hours. Taste for seasoning and add salt and pepper if necessary.

Transfer the chili to serving bowls and garnish with lime wedges, sour cream, shredded cheese and sliced scallions.

MANZANITA CREEK

This is a recipe I adapted from a little restaurant in Los Gatos, my old stomping grounds. The dish was a hearty crowd pleaser in the 1980s. Nancy used to work the graveyard shift in the emergency room at Kaiser Santa Clara; thanks to my Sicilian upbringing, I'm a cooking fool, and fed the family during those years while Nancy worked nights. Contadina in Italian means female farmer; I should probably call this recipe "New Contadino!"

1441 A-B Grove Street
Healdsburg, CA 95448
707-433-4052
manzanitacreek.com

NEW CONTADINA

chef Jack Salerno

Pair with Manzanita Creek Cloud Buster Russian River Valley Zinfandel

SERVES 8

1-1/2 pounds potatoes, peeled
and cut into 1-1/2-inch cubes
1 pound ziti or penne pasta
3/4 cup olive oil
5 links Silva brand sweet
Italian sausage, sliced
1/4-inch thick diagonally
2 large red bell peppers,
cut in 1/2-inch strips
1 pound grape tomatoes,
sliced in half
1/4 cup Italian parsley,
chopped
1 teaspoon red pepper flakes
Pecorino Romano, grated,
for garnish

In a large pot, bring 2 gallons of water to a boil. Add a very generous amount of sea salt or kosher salt. Add the potatoes and boil them until they're just firm, 8 to 10 minutes. Remove the potatoes from the pot with a slotted spoon and place them in a bowl. Set aside.

Add the pasta to the boiling water and cook it for 10 minutes, or until it's firm to the bite. Drain all but 1 cup of the water from the pot and add 1/4 cup olive oil to prevent the pasta from sticking.

In a 10-inch sauté pan, cook the sausages over medium heat, turning them only once; pierce the skin with a knife to allow the fat to drain as they cook. Add 1/4 cup water to the pan after 5 minutes to keep the sausages from burning; you want them browned. Allow them to cool.

In a 14-inch pan, heat the remaining 1/2 cup of olive oil, add the bell peppers and a pinch of salt, and cook until the peppers are tender, about 15 minutes. Add the tomatoes and another pinch of salt. Cook until the mixture thickens a bit. Add the potatoes and cook 5 minutes more, so that the potatoes absorb the liquid. Add the pasta and sausage, heat through, then add the parsley and red pepper flakes. Adjust the seasoning with salt and pepper if necessary.

Transfer the mixture to a large serving plate, and either sprinkle the grated Pecorino Romano on top, or make it available in a small bowl.

MARTINELLI WINERY

Charles Ranch, our property just two miles inland from the Pacific Ocean at Fort Ross, was first homesteaded in the 1860s by Carolyn Martinelli's family. This property has always been ideally suited to hunting wild boar and deer for venison. At many family gatherings and special occasions, we would enjoy Carolyn's Wild Game Stew; now we hope you do as well.

3360 River Road
Windsor, CA 95492
707-525-0570
martinelliwinery.com

WILD GAME STEW

chef Dianne Martin

Pair with Martinelli Terra Felice Syrah

SERVES 6-8

2 pounds venison or beef
   stew meat

2 tablespoons olive oil

sea salt to taste

2 teaspoons pepper

2 tablespoons dried
   rosemary

2 tablespoons dried thyme

2 large yellow onions,
   chopped

1 to 2 small cans tomato paste

1 small can water (use the
   tomato paste can)

1 cup beef broth

1 pepperwood tree leaf

²/₃ bottle Martinelli Syrah

Cut the meat into 1-1/2-inch pieces. Heat the olive oil in a sauté pan and add the meat. Sprinkle with the salt, pepper, rosemary and thyme and cook, stirring frequently, on medium heat.

In another small pan, sauté the onions lightly, then add them to the meat. Lower the heat to low and continue to cook the mixture until the meat is browned on all sides. Add the tomato paste, water and broth, stir well, then add the pepperwood tree leaf. Simmer the stew, covered, for at least 4 hours. If too much liquid remains at the end of that time, remove the lid and cook the stew down a bit more.

We like to serve the stew over hot polenta; the Golden Pheasant brand is recommended. Just follow the directions on the box.

MATRIX WINERY

Chef Bruce Riezenman says cassoulet was one of the first recipes he learned during his culinary training, and it became one of his favorites. Making the traditional recipe is a long, slow process, so Bruce created a simpler version to share — one that doesn't take all day to prepare, yet retains the same delicious flavors found in the slow-cooked version. The earthiness of the mushrooms and the smoky bacon flavors echo our Pinot Noir's earth notes and complement the dark, rich fruit flavors.

3291 Westside Road
Healdsburg, CA 95448
707-433-1911
matrixwinery.com

duck & pork
CASSOULET

chef Bruce Riezenman, Park Avenue Catering

Pair with Matrix Russian River Valley Pinot Noir

SERVES 8-10

3/4 pound pork shoulder, trimmed of fat and cubed

3 teaspoons kosher salt

6 ounces bacon, diced

6 cloves garlic, peeled and sliced

1-1/2 cups yellow onions, diced

1 cup carrots, peeled and diced

18 grinds black pepper

3 teaspoons herbs de Provence

1-1/2 cups crimini mushrooms, diced

1-1/2 cups canned diced tomatoes, strained of juice

5 cups chicken stock

1 pound mild Italian sausage, cooked, skinned and chopped

2 quarts white beans, cooked

1 pound duck confit meat, skin, fat and bones removed, cut into large chunks

2 cups panko bread crumbs or any unflavored bread crumbs

Preheat oven to 375°.

In a bowl, toss the cubed pork with 1 teaspoon of kosher salt and let sit for 20 minutes.

Meanwhile, place the bacon in a heavy-bottomed, 5-quart sauce pot over medium heat. Cover the pot and cook the bacon, stirring occasionally, until the fat is rendered and the bacon is golden and crisp. Remove the bacon from the pan and set it aside.

Increase the heat to medium-high and add the pork to the hot bacon fat. Brown the pork, then remove it from the pan and set it aside.

Reduce the heat to medium and add the bacon, garlic, onions and carrots into the pan with the bacon fat. Add the remainder of the salt, the pepper and the herbs de Provence. Cover the pot and sweat the vegetables until they're soft, stirring occasionally. Add the mushrooms and cook for 5 minutes.

Add the rest of the ingredients except the bread crumbs. Bring the mixture to a simmer, then transfer it to an 11-inch by 15-inch ceramic baking dish, or two baking dishes large enough to hold all the ingredients.

Bake the cassoulet for 30 minutes, uncovered, until the top is crusted. Stir the cassoulet to fold the crust into the mixture, and bake for another 30 minutes. Stir again. Top the cassoulet with the bread crumbs and bake for 30 more minutes, until the crumbs begin to turn golden and form a nice crust on top.

Allow the cassoulet to cool for a few minutes, and serve it with sautéed chard.

MAZZOCCO SONOMA

"Short ribs have a great combination of richness, taste and texture," says chef Bruce Riezenman. "During the summer I grill them, but when the weather turns cold, there is nothing quite like a braised short rib and a glass of Zinfandel." Start this recipe one day ahead.

1400 Lytton Springs Road
Healdsburg, CA 95448
707-431-8159
mazzocco.com

beef
SHORT RIBS
with zinfandel-maple reduction sauce

chef Bruce Riezenman, Park Avenue Catering

Pair with Mazzocco Dry Creek Valley Zinfandel

SERVES 4

2 tablespoons canola oil

3-1/2 pounds beef short ribs (4 pieces cut 1-1/2 inches thick)

salt and pepper to taste

1 tablespoon olive oil

2 tablespoons butter

1/2 onion, diced

1 clove garlic, crushed

1 carrot, peeled and diced

1 celery stalk, peeled and diced

3/4 cup Zinfandel

1/2 cup chicken broth

3/4 cup veal or beef broth

18 juniper berries, crushed

4 bay leaves

8 thyme sprigs

2 tablespoons maple syrup

1 teaspoon Maldon sea salt or kosher salt

Prepare the ribs one day in advance by preheating the oven to 350°.

Pour the canola oil into a 10-inch cast-iron skillet and heat it over a medium flame. Season the beef with salt and pepper. When the oil is hot, but before it starts to smoke, add the short ribs and sear them until they're brown on all sides — about 8 minutes.

Lower the heat and remove the beef from the pan. Add the olive oil and butter, then the onions, garlic, carrots and celery. Add a pinch of salt, then stir and cover. Cook the vegetables for 4 to 5 minutes, until the onions start to soften.

Add the Zinfandel and turn the heat to medium-high. Reduce the wine by half, and add the chicken broth, veal broth, 1/2 of the juniper berries, the bay leaves and the thyme. Bring the mixture to a simmer, and return the beef to the pan. Cover the pan and place it in the oven for 1 to 1-1/2 hours, until the rib meat is tender.

You should have 1 to 1-1/2 cups of sauce remaining in the pan. Place the short ribs and this sauce in a glass baking dish, let them cool, and chill them in the refrigerator overnight.

The next day, remove the fat that has risen to the top of the sauce. Scrape the excess sauce off the beef and into a small saucepan. Add the maple syrup, simmer the sauce, and season with salt and pepper to taste.

Crush the rest of the juniper berries and coat the short ribs in them. Sear the ribs in a cast-iron skillet, turning them carefully so they do not fall apart. Serve the warm short ribs over celery root mashed potatoes and pour the sauce over the meat and mash. Top with a sprinkle of Maldon sea salt.

MERRIAM VINEYARDS

Josh Silvers walks into a bar with a duck on his head. The bartender says, "Where did you get the drunken chef?" Josh says, "He's not a drunken chef, he's a duck and I think he's sober." Bartender says, "I was talking to the duck." Seriously, though, we wanted a dish that would pair with our Cabernet Franc, one that is elegant and powerful, and also comfortable. Josh's suggestion of duck, orange, dried cherries, onion and carrots had us salivating, and we knew we had our match.

11654 Los Amigos Road
Healdsburg, CA 95448
707-433-4032
merriamvineyards.com

josh silvers'
DRUNKEN DUCK

chef Josh Silvers, Jackson's Bar and Oven

Pair with Merriam Vineyards Windacre Vineyard Cabernet Franc

SERVES 6-8

DUCK

1 cinnamon stick

3 cloves

1 orange (organic), with a 4-inch by 1-inch zest strip

2 sprigs thyme

1 bay leaf

6 large duck legs

3 cups Merriam Cabernet Franc

1 cup Merriam Late Harvest Cabernet Franc (or port)

1 tablespoon vegetable oil

1 large carrot, roughly chopped

1 large celery rib, roughly chopped

1 large onion, roughly chopped

1 tablespoon tomato paste

2 large fresh flat-leaf parsley sprigs

1 cup chicken stock

1 cup dried cherries

2 tablespoons cold butter

Prepare a bouquet garni by tying the cinnamon stick, cloves, orange zest, thyme and bay leaf in a cheesecloth bag.

Preheat the oven to 350°.

Trim any excess fat from the duck legs and freeze the fat for use later. Marinate the duck legs and bouquet garni in the wine for 2 hours. Remove the duck from the marinade and pat the legs dry. Heat the oil in a heavy braising pan. Season the legs with salt and begin browning them, skin side down, until they reach a mahogany color and the skin is crisp. Turn the legs over and brown the other side, then remove them to paper towels. Pour off the fat and save it for another use.

In the same pan, sauté the carrot, celery and onion. When they start to brown, add the tomato paste and cook for 2 minutes on medium heat, then add the duck legs (skin side up), parsley sprigs, chicken stock, juice from the orange, marinade and the bouquet garni. Bring the ingredients to a simmer, cover the braising pan and place it in the preheated oven for 1-1/2 hours, or until the meat is tender.

Remove the duck legs to a plate and cover to keep them warm. Using a ladle or large spoon, remove as much fat as you can from the braising pan, then strain the contents into a small pot. Add the cherries and reduce until the sauce starts to thicken. Whisk in the butter. Pour the sauce over the duck legs and serve over wild rice or lentils.

MILL CREEK VINEYARDS

This is Ken Rochioli's grandmother's recipe. It was an integral part of large, warm family get-togethers, which included lively talk, delicious food, abundant wine and the creation of happy childhood memories.

1401 Westside Road
Healdsburg, CA 95448
707-431-2121
millcreekwinery.com

nonna's
ITALIAN MEATBALLS

chef Ken Rochioli, KR Catering

Pair with Mill Creek Dry Creek Valley Zinfandel

SERVES 4

MEATBALLS

⅓ cup bread crumbs

3 tablespoons milk

⅓ cup fresh Parmesan cheese

¼ cup onion, finely chopped

3 tablespoons fresh basil, chopped

1 egg

3 cloves garlic, minced

½ teaspoon ground black pepper

8 ounces bulk Italian sausage

8 ounces ground beef

2 tablespoons pine nuts

2 tablespoons dried currants

SAUCE

1 tablespoon olive oil

¾ cup onion, chopped

2 garlic cloves, minced

1 28-ounce can diced tomatoes

4 tablespoons fresh basil, chopped

To prepare the meatballs, preheat the oven to 350°.

Mix the bread crumbs and milk in a medium bowl and let them stand for 5 minutes. Add the Parmesan, onions, basil, egg, garlic, pepper, sausage, ground beef, pine nuts and currants, and blend well. Using wet hands, form the mixture into balls. Sauté the meatballs in a nonstick pan over medium heat until they're uniformly browned. Place them on a baking sheet and bake for 10 minutes.

To prepare the sauce, heat the oil in large, heavy-bottom pot over medium-low heat. Add the onions and sauté until they're golden, approximately 10 minutes. Add the garlic, stir the pot for 1 minute, then add the tomatoes and their juice, and half of the basil, and bring them to a boil. Reduce the heat and simmer the sauce until it thickens – about 1 hour — breaking up the tomatoes with a fork. Mix in the remaining basil and season with salt and pepper.

Add the meatballs to the pot, warm them through, and serve.

MOSHIN VINEYARDS

Wild mushrooms begin to make their appearance in late October/early November, and Sonoma County has all sorts from which to choose. The earthiness of the mushrooms brings out the depth of Russian River Pinot Noir, and the star anise enhances the wine's perfume. We prefer organically raised Liberty Ducks from Petaluma.

10295 Westside Road
Healdsburg, CA 95448
707-433-5499
moshinvineyards.com

roast duck
BREAD PUDDING

Recipe by Mat Gustafson, prepared by chef Dan Lucia

Pair with Moshin Vineyards Russian River Valley Pinot Noir

SERVES 8-10

10 star anise

3 cups duck stock
  (or chicken stock)

6 brioche rolls

2 medium leeks, white and
  light green parts only,
  sliced 1/2-inch thick

4 tablespoons unsalted butter

8 ounces fresh wild
  mushrooms, cleaned and
  chopped

1-1/2 cups roasted duck meat,
  shredded

1 tablespoon fresh thyme,
  finely chopped

1 cup Emmentaler cheese,
  shredded

3 large eggs

3 cups heavy cream

pinch nutmeg

salt and pepper to taste

Preheat oven to 350°.

Place the star anise and duck stock in a saucepan and simmer for 30 minutes. Remove and discard the star anise, and allow the stock to cool completely.

Cut the brioche into 1/2-inch cubes, place them on a sheet pan, and toast them in the oven until they're dry and just browning, about 15 minutes.

In a medium sauté pan with a lid, cook the leeks over low to medium heat for 5 minutes to soften and release their liquid, stirring often to prevent browning. Add the butter to the pan, stir to emulsify, and then add the chopped mushrooms. Cover the pan with the lid slightly ajar, and cook for 30 minutes, or until the leeks are very soft.

In a large bowl, toss together the toasted bread cubes, leeks, mushrooms and shredded duck meat. Add the thyme and cheese, mix well, and set aside.

In another large bowl, whisk the eggs until they're smooth. Add the cream, cooled stock, nutmeg, salt and pepper, and mix until smooth. Spread the bread/duck mixture in a 9-inch by 13-inch baking pan, pour the egg mixture over it, and let it soak for 15 minutes. Bake for 1-1/2 hours or until the pudding is set and the top is browned, then serve.

MUELLER WINERY

Thanks to chef Shari from Baci Café & Wine Bar for this deliciously rich creation. We asked Shari to come up with something special to serve at our 20th anniversary Mueller Winemaker Dinner in May 2012. We knew it had to include his Emily's Cuvée Pinot Noir Reduction Sauce and creamy polenta, but the rest was up to him. Shari's meals have revived us more than once during late harvest nights.

6301 Starr Road
Windsor, CA 95492
707-837-7399
muellerwine.com

DUCK CONFIT
with emily's cuvée reduction & creamy polenta

chef Shari Sarabi, Baci Café & Wine Bar

Pair with Mueller Russian River Valley Pinot Noir

SERVES 6

DUCK

3 ounces kosher salt
2 ounces light brown sugar
2 ounces black peppercorns
¼ tablespoon ground nutmeg
¼ tablespoon ground cinnamon
¼ tablespoon ground cloves
6 fatty duck legs
2 quarts duck fat
1 bottle Mueller Emily's Cuvée
   Pinot Noir
2 cups demi-glace
½ teaspoon fresh thyme
1 clove garlic, minced
1 shallot, minced
1 stick butter
salt and pepper to taste

POLENTA

1 tablespoon olive oil
1 medium yellow onion, finely diced
1 tablespoon garlic, minced
1 teaspoon rosemary
½ cup polenta
3 cups chicken stock
1 cup heavy cream
½ cup Parmesan cheese, grated
¼ pound butter

To prepare the confit, begin the recipe 48 hours ahead.

In a small bowl, combine the first 6 ingredients (through cloves). Rub the duck legs well with the mixture, and place them in a glass baking dish. Cover the dish with foil, and place a heavy plate or other weight on top. Refrigerate the duck for 48 hours.

When you're ready to cook the duck, rinse the legs well and pat them dry. Place the duck fat in a large saucepan and bring it to a simmer. Add the legs, making sure they are completely submerged in the fat. Cover the top of the pan with parchment paper, and let the legs simmer for 3 to 4 hours, or until they're fork-tender. Allow the duck to cool to room temperature, remove the skin and bone, and shred the meat. Keep it warm.

Prepare the Pinot Noir reduction sauce by pouring the wine into a saucepan. Over medium heat, reduce the liquid to 1/3. Add the demi-glace, thyme, garlic and shallot, then blend in the butter. Season the sauce with salt and pepper and strain it before serving.

To prepare the polenta, heat the oil in a large sauté pan. Add the onion, garlic and rosemary, and cook until the onions are translucent. Add 1 cup of the chicken stock and the cream, and bring the mixture to a boil. Reduce the heat and add the polenta, whisking until it's smooth. On low heat, cook the polenta for 30 minutes, frequently but slowly adding the remaining chicken stock so that the polenta does not get thick. Remove the polenta from the heat and add the butter and Parmesan cheese while whisking.

Serve the duck confit on top of the polenta and drizzle with the reduction sauce.

OLD WORLD WINERY

It was during a work party that we fell in love with this hearty yet luxurious meatloaf sandwich. We like to serve it on ciabatta rolls.

850 River Road
Fulton, CA 95439
707-490-6696
oldworldwinery.com

MEATLOAF
with pancetta & shiitake mushrooms

chef Helena Gustavsson Giesea

Pair with Old World Fulton Folderol

SERVES 4-6

1 tablespoon olive oil
1/4 cup yellow onion, chopped
1/4 cup carrot, small dice
1/4 cup celery, small dice
2 pounds grass-fed lean
  sirloin, ground
1/2 cup cooked pancetta,
  chopped
1/2 cup shiitake mushrooms,
  chopped
1 cup bread crumbs
1/2 cup whole milk
2 eggs
3 tablespoons Dijon mustard
3 tablespoons
  Worchestershire sauce
1/4 cup chili sauce
1 tablespoon sea salt
1 tablespoon black pepper
3 tablespoons paprika
ciabatta rolls

Preheat the oven to 400°.

Heat the olive oil in a sauté pan and cook the onion, carrot and celery until they're tender.

In a large bowl, add the remaining ingredients and mix well. Press the meat mixture into a greased baking dish, and bake the loaf for 40 to 60 minutes, until it's cooked through.

Let the meatloaf loaf rest for 10 minutes before removing it from the baking dish. Slice the loaf to the desired thickness and serve the slices on ciabatta rolls.

PAPAPIETRO PERRY

This recipe came about as we talked about our favorite comfort foods from our childhood. Nothing warmed the tummy and heart quite like a piping-hot chicken pot pie. As we've evolved into foodies, we wondered how we could make the ultimate pot pie that would pair beautifully with our Pinot Noirs, and pork and pancetta came up again and again as ingredients. The result is this recipe; be sure to start it one day in advance.

4791 Dry Creek Road, Building #4
Healdsburg, CA 95448
707-433-0422
papapietro-perry.com

pork & pancetta
POT PIE

chef Bruce Riezenman, Park Avenue Catering

Pair with Papapietro Perry Russian River Valley Pinot Noir

SERVES 8

1 tablespoon canola oil

$^1/_4$ pound pancetta, diced

1-$^1/_2$ pounds pork shoulder, cleaned, fat removed and diced ($^1/_2$-inch)

6 ounces yellow onions, diced

4 ounces celery, diced

6 ounces carrots, peeled and diced

1 tablespoon butter

6 ounces mushrooms, diced

1 teaspoon cardamom, ground

1-$^1/_2$ teaspoons gumbo filé

1/8 teaspoon cayenne pepper

1 teaspoon espelette powder

$^1/_4$ teaspoon cloves, ground

$^1/_4$ teaspoon nutmeg, ground

3 teaspoons kosher salt

$^1/_2$ cup Sherry wine, pale dry

2 cups chicken broth

4 ounces celery root, diced

6 ounces Yukon Gold potatoes, diced

6 ounces peas

1 ounce parsley

$^1/_2$ ounce thyme

pie dough

BECHAMEL

1-$^1/_2$ tablespoons butter

$^1/_4$ cup flour

2 cups cold milk

Place the canola oil and pancetta in a heavy-bottomed skillet over medium heat. Cover the skillet and render the pancetta until it's crisp. Remove the pancetta to paper towels to drain, and add the pork pieces, browning them on all sides. Remove the pork to paper towels (do this in 2 or 3 batches).

Add the onions, celery and carrots. Cover the skillet and reduce the heat to medium-low. Cook the vegetables for 5 minutes, stirring occasionally. Add the mushrooms, spices, herbs and salt. Cover and cook for 8 to 10 minutes, stirring occasionally. Add the Sherry, raise the heat to medium-high and reduce the wine to 1/2. Add the pork, pancetta and chicken broth. Simmer the mixture, covered, for 30 minutes.

Meanwhile, prepare the béchamel sauce. Melt the butter in a heavy-bottomed saucepan over low heat. Add the flour and mix well. Cook the roux for 5 minutes over low heat. Remove the pan from heat, let the mixture cool slightly, and add 1/4 cup of the milk. Mix together until you have a smooth paste. Return the pan to low-medium heat and add more milk, 1/4 cup at a time, mixing each time to make sure it is smooth. Simmer the sauce until it thickens.

To the simmering pot of pork, add the celery root, potatoes, peas and béchamel. Simmer the contents uncovered for 20 minutes, or until the pork is tender. Season with salt and pepper as needed, and let the mixture cool overnight in the refrigerator.

The next day, preheat the oven to 375°. Place the pot pie filling in a casserole dish and top it with your favorite pie dough. Score the top of the dough with 3 slits, and bake the pie until the crust is cooked through and the filling is bubbling.

PEDRONCELLI WINERY

We wanted to focus on one of our estate wines for this recipe. Our Sangiovese is a very versatile wine; we often refer to it as a "favorite pair of slippers" wine — you just slip into it at the end of a long day because it is uncomplicated and ready to pair with anything from meatloaf to margherita pizza. This spicy, full-flavored dish is from Anna Beth and Vince Chao from epicurious.com.

1220 Canyon Road
Geyserville, CA 95441
800-836-3894
pedroncelli.com

chicken & sausage
JAMBALAYA

Pair with Pedroncelli Alto Vineyards Dry Creek Valley Sangiovese

SERVES 18-24

12 ounces applewood-smoked bacon, diced

1-1/2 pounds smoked, fully cooked sausage, halved lengthwise, cut crosswise into 1/2-inch-thick semi-circles

1 pound andouille sausage, quartered lengthwise, cut crosswise into 1/2-inch cubes

1/2 pound tasso or smoked ham, cut into 1/2-inch cubes

1-1/2 pounds onions, chopped

2 large celery stalks, chopped

2 red bell peppers, coarsely chopped

6 large skinless, boneless chicken thighs, cut into 1-inch pieces

2 tablespoons paprika

1 tablespoon fresh thyme, chopped

1 tablespoon chili powder

1/4 teaspoon (or more) cayenne pepper

3 10-ounce cans diced tomatoes with green chiles

2-1/2 cups beef broth

3 cups long-grain white rice

8 green onions, chopped

fresh Italian parsley, chopped

Position a rack in the bottom third of the oven and preheat to 350°.

Cook the bacon in a very large, oven-proof pot over medium-high heat until the bacon is brown but not yet crisp, stirring often. Add the smoked sausage, andouille and tasso/ham. Sauté the meats until they start to brown in spots, about 10 minutes.

Add the onions, celery and bell peppers, and cook until they begin to soften, stirring occasionally, 10 to 12 minutes. Mix in the chicken and continue to cook until the outside of the meat turns white, stirring often, 5 to 6 minutes. Mix in the paprika, thyme, chili powder and cayenne and cook for 1 minute. Add the tomatoes with chiles and the broth; stir to blend well. Add more cayenne, if desired, then mix in the rice.

Bring the jambalaya to a boil and cover the pot. Place it in the oven and bake the mixture until the rice is tender and the liquids are absorbed, 45 to 48 minutes. Uncover the pot, mix in the green onions, sprinkle the jambalaya with the chopped parsley, and serve.

RIDGE VINEYARDS

These malfatti, which literally means "badly made" in Italian, are extraordinarily delicious, sexy ricotta cheese dumplings bathed in a hearty meat sauce. The "badly made" name is said to have emerged when an Italian chef ended up with extra ravioli filling and cleverly turned it into dumplings.

650 Lytton Springs Road
Healdsburg, CA 95448
707-433-7721
ridgewine.com

RICOTTA MALFATTI
with sweet italian sausage, spinach & peppers

Pair with Ridge Lytton Springs Zinfandel

SERVES 6-8

SAUCE

2 pounds bulk sweet Italian sausage, rolled into 1-inch balls

3 tablespoons extra-virgin olive oil, plus more for brushing

2 red bell peppers, cut into 1-inch dice

2 green bell peppers, cut into 1-inch dice

2 yellow bell peppers, cut into 1-inch dice

1 medium red onion, thinly sliced

1 small fennel bulb, trimmed, cored and thinly sliced

4 serrano chiles, seeded and thinly sliced crosswise

1 habanero chile, seeded and thinly sliced

2 cups Ridge Lytton Springs Zinfandel

2 cups baby spinach

1.5 ounces freshly grated pecorino cheese

MALFATTI

3/4 cup canola/olive oil blend

1/2 cup shallots, minced

1/4 cup garlic, minced

3 pounds fresh ricotta cheese

3 extra-large eggs

1/2 cup Italian parsley, roughly chopped

1/2 cup chives, minced

kosher salt and white pepper to taste

3 to 4 cups all-purpose flour

1.5 ounces freshly grated pecorino cheese

To prepare the sauce, heat a cast-iron skillet over medium-high heat for 10 minutes. Add the sausage balls and cook them for 2 minutes, shaking the skillet so that they brown on all sides. Remove the sausage balls and set them aside.

Drain the oil from the skillet, wipe it clean with paper towels, and reheat the pan over medium-high heat. Add the 3 tablespoons of olive oil, peppers, onion, fennel and chiles and cook, stirring occasionally, until the vegetables are softened, about 15 minutes. Season them with salt.

Add the sausages and wine to the skillet and simmer until the wine has reduced by half, about 4 minutes. Remove the skillet from the heat and fold in the spinach. Sprinkle 1.5 ounces of the cheese over the mixture.

To prepare the malfatti, heat the oil blend in a skillet, add the shallots and garlic, and sauté until they're translucent. Add the vegetables to a mixer bowl, along with the ricotta, eggs, parsley and chives. Mix together with the paddle attachment just until the ingredients are incorporated. Add half of the flour to the bowl and mix at medium speed. Pulse to incorporate the flour, turn off the mixer, and add the remaining flour. Pulse again until the flour is incorporated.

Using a tablespoon, scoop the dough into balls and place them on a lightly floured surface. Bring to boil 1 gallon of water. Add 1 tablespoon of salt to the water. Gently place the balls into the water and boil them gently for 10 minutes, or until they float. Once they float, cook them an additional 3 to 5 minutes. Drain the dumplings, toss them with a little olive oil, and serve them with the sauce and crusty sourdough bread. Pass the remaining pecorino cheese at the table.

ROADHOUSE WINERY

Our tasting room is next door to Oakville Grocery, where they make wonderful pizzas. Aubrey McMinn is the catering manager there, and created this pizza to go with our Dry Creek Zinfandel. The Margherita is topped with modest amounts of tomato sauce, mozzarella cheese and fresh basil, and represents the three colors of the Italian flag: red, white and green.

240 Center Street
Healdsburg, Ca 95448
707-922-6362
roadhousewinery.com

MARGHERITA PIZZA

chef Aubrey McMinn, Oakville Grocery

Pair with Roadhouse Winery Dry Creek Valley Zinfandel

SERVES 8

SAUCE
1 tablespoon olive oil
1/2 yellow onion, diced
4 garlic cloves, minced
1 tablespoon salt
1 tablespoon Italian seasoning
1 tablespoon sugar
1 28-ounce can tomato puree
1 28-ounce can diced tomatoes
6 basil leaves, chopped

DOUGH
1 cup warm water (110°)
1 packet dry yeast
  (about .25 ounce)
1 teaspoon granulated sugar
2-1/2 cups all-purpose flour
2 tablespoons extra-virgin olive oil
1 teaspoon salt

TOPPINGS
4-ounce ball fresh mozzarella
  cheese, sliced
1 fresh tomato, chopped
6 garlic cloves, roasted and gently
  sliced
1/2 bunch basil, chopped
1/4 cup Parmesan cheese, grated

Begin by preparing the tomato sauce. Heat the oil in a sauté pan and add the onion, garlic, salt and Italian seasoning. Cook over medium heat until the vegetables are golden brown. Add the sugar and the cans of tomato puree and diced tomatoes, and simmer the mixture on low for 30 minutes. Add the basil and puree the sauce in a blender. Set the sauce aside to cool.

To prepare the dough, preheat the oven to 450°. In a medium bowl, dissolve the yeast and sugar in the warm water and let it stand for 10 minutes. Stir in the flour, oil and salt, and beat the mixture until it's smooth. Let the dough rest for 7 minutes on the counter.

Place the dough on a floured surface, and pat or roll it into a round shape. Place the dough on a lightly oiled pizza pan or cookie sheet. Add the sauce and toppings, and bake the pizza for 15 to 20 minutes.

ROBERT YOUNG ESTATE WINERY

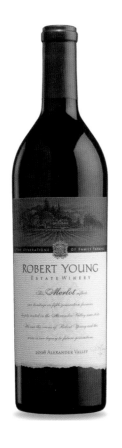

Fifty years ago a young South African visited our ranch. Since that chance meeting, we've hosted more than 400 South Africans and created friendships that span three generations. These traditional Boerewors sausages are now a cherished family recipe. Start the sausages one day in advance.

4960 Red Winery Road
Geyserville, CA 95441
707-431-4811
ryew.com

south african-style
BOEREWORS SAUSAGES
with merlot-caramelized onions

chef JoAnn Young & Park Avenue Catering

Pair with Robert Young Estate Winery Merlot

MAKES 36 SAUSAGES

SAUSAGES

3 pounds coarse-ground beef
   (18% to 20% fat)
4-1/4 pounds coarse-ground pork butt
   (very fatty)
1 pound lamb shoulder, coarse-ground
3 tablespoons white vinegar
1/3 cup ground coriander
1 tablespoon pickling spice,
   ground fine
1/2 teaspoon ground nutmeg
3 tablespoons brown sugar
3 tablespoons salt
1-1/2 teaspoons garlic salt
1 tablespoon black pepper,
   medium grind
1/4 teaspoon cayenne pepper
1/4 teaspoon ground cloves
1/4 pound pork sausage casings

ONIONS

6 cups red onions, peeled and
   thinly sliced
2 cups Merlot or other full-bodied
   red wine
1/2 cup sugar
2 bay leaves
1/8 teaspoon cayenne pepper
2 tablespoons balsamic vinegar
pinch salt

Begin preparing the sausages 1 day ahead. Cut the meats into cubes and place the cubes in a large bowl. Add the remaining ingredients except for the casings and mix well. Cover the bowl and place it in the refrigerator overnight, so that the ingredients marry and marinate the meat.

The next day, grind the meat mixture on a coarse setting — 1/4-inch is ideal. Stuff the seasoned meat into the sausage casings and tie each link off in the length you like.

Before you cook the sausages, prepare the Merlot-caramelized onions. In a heavy-bottom saucepan, place the onions, wine, sugar and bay leaves. Cover the pan tightly and simmer the ingredients for 15 minutes over medium-high heat. Uncover the pan and continue cooking for about 45 minutes, stirring occasionally, until most of the liquid has evaporated. Season to taste with salt.

Grill the sausages and serve them with the warm Merlot-caramelized onions.

ROUTE 128 WINERY

We continue our tradition of serving one of nephew Rian Rinn's delicious dishes. This creative recipe wowed us at one wintry Opatz family dinner, when Pete poured the Opatz Family Syrah with chef Rian's savory meal.

21079 Geyserville Avenue
Geyserville, CA 95441
707-696-0004
route128winery.com

braised
PORK SHANK
with apricots

chef Rian Rinn

Pair with Route 128 Syrah

SERVES 6

1 tablespoon peanut oil
6 pieces pork shank, skin
  on, 2 inches thick (ask your
  butcher for osso buco cut)
2 large carrots, 1/8-inch dice
1 large onion, 1/8-inch dice
2 garlic cloves, crushed
10 whole black peppercorns
1 bay leaf
1 bottle Route 128 Syrah
6 cups chicken stock
1 tablespoon olive oil
1/2 pound apricots
1 teaspoon fresh thyme
1 teaspoon ground coriander
1/8 teaspoon grated licorice
  root
1/8 teaspoon cayenne pepper
salt and pepper to taste

Preheat the oven to 350°.

To a large cast-iron skillet, add the peanut oil and warm it over medium heat. Season the pork shanks with salt, place them in the skillet and sear them until they're golden brown on both sides. Remove the shanks from the pan and pour off the fat.

Add the carrots, onion, garlic, peppercorns and bay leaf to the skillet. Sauté the vegetables until they're soft; do not caramelize or brown them. Return the shanks to the skillet, add 3/4 bottle of the Syrah and cook until the liquid is reduced by 1/2. Add the chicken stock. Place the skillet in the oven, uncovered, for 1-1/2 hours, or until the liquid begins to appear glossy.

In a separate pan, add the olive oil and heat until the oil smokes. Add the apricots, thyme, coriander, licorice root and cayenne. Brown these ingredients and deglaze the pan with the remainder of the Syrah. Add the apricot mixture to the pork shanks and serve.

RUED VINEYARDS

This rustic yet creamy lasagna is perfect with a glass of Rued Zinfandel on a cool fall evening.

3850 Dry Creek Road
Healdsburg, CA 95448
707-433-3261
ruedvineyards.com

spinach & portobello
MUSHROOM LASAGNA

vegi

chef Randi Kauppi

Pair with Rued Vineyards Dry Creek Valley Zinfandel

SERVES 10

1 8-ounce package uncooked
   lasagna noodles
1 teaspoon olive oil
7 cups sliced baby portobello
   mushrooms (about 1 pound)
3 cups white mushrooms,
   sliced
½ teaspoon ground nutmeg
3 garlic cloves, minced
2 15-ounce containers ricotta
   cheese
2 10-ounce packages frozen
   chopped spinach, thawed,
   drained and squeezed dry
¼ cup Parmesan cheese,
   grated
1 teaspoon dried Italian
   seasoning
1 teaspoon pepper
3-½ cups marinara sauce
cooking spray
3 cups mozzarella cheese,
   grated

Cook the lasagna noodles according to the package directions. Drain the noodles and set 9 of them aside.

Heat the oil in a nonstick skillet over medium heat. Add the mushrooms and sauté them for 3 minutes. Add the nutmeg and garlic, and continue to sauté for 5 minutes. Set the mushrooms aside.

Combine the ricotta, spinach, Parmesan, Italian seasoning and pepper in a large bowl; set it aside.

Preheat the oven to 375°.

Spread 1/2 cup of marinara sauce in the bottom of a 13-inch by 9-inch baking dish coated with cooking spray. Arrange 3 lasagna noodles over the sauce, and top them with 1/2 the ricotta cheese mixture, 1/2 of the mushroom mixture, 1-1/2 cups of marinara and 1 cup of mozzarella. Repeat the layering, ending with noodles. Spread 1/2 cup of sauce over the top layer of the noodles.

Cover and bake the lasagna for 40 minutes. Uncover the lasagna, sprinkle the remaining mozzarella and Parmesan cheeses over the top, and bake 10 minutes more, uncovered. Let the lasagna stand 10 minutes before serving.

RUSSIAN HILL ESTATE WINERY

Lamb and Syrah is one of the great pairings in the cuisine of southern France. As producers of Syrah, we are always looking for new and creative ways to match these two great foods (yes, we think of wine as food!). Chef Renée Pisan came up with the perfect flavors to add to lamb - olives and oranges - to highlight our Top Block Syrah.

4525 Slusser Road
Windsor, CA 95492
707-575-9428
russianhillestate.com

provençal
LAMB DAUBE
with red wine, olives & oranges

chef Renée Pisan, Chloe's French Café

Pair with Russian Hill Top Block Syrah

SERVES 8-10

3 pounds boneless lamb shoulder, cut into 2-inch pieces
sea salt
course-ground black pepper
3 tablespoons olive oil
1 tablespoon butter
1 medium yellow onion, large dice
3 medium carrots, large dice
4 cloves garlic, chopped
1 tablespoon tomato paste
1 tablespoon brown sugar
2 tablespoons all-purpose flour
2 cups Syrah
1 cup chicken stock
1 orange, zest, pulp and juice (reserve some zest for garnish)
1 bouquet garni (2 bay leaves, 2 thyme sprigs, 1 rosemary sprig, 6 juniper berries, 1 teaspoon dried peppercorns, pinch of dried lavender buds, tied together in cheesecloth)
2 potatoes, large dice
½ cup pitted green olives
2 sprigs flat-leaf parsley
1 sprig rosemary
1 sprig thyme, finely chopped together with the reserved orange zest for garnish

Season the lamb with sea salt and pepper. Heat the olive oil and butter in a Dutch oven on high heat. Add the lamb pieces, in batches, and sear them until they're browned and caramelized. Remove them from the pan and set aside.

To the hot pan, add the onion and carrots and cook over medium-high heat until they caramelize. Add the garlic and cook for 1 minute. Stir in the tomato paste, brown sugar and flour, and cook for 2 to 3 minutes. Add the wine, chicken stock and orange zest, pulp and juice, while scraping the bottom of the pan to lift the brown bits into the daube.

Add the lamb and the bouquet garni to the pot and bring the mixture to a boil. Cover the pot and reduce the liquid over very low heat for approximately 1-1/2 hours. Stir every 30 minutes, skimming the fat from the surface as needed.

When the lamb is fork-tender, remove the bouquet garni, add the potatoes and olives, and cook for 15 minutes more, or until the potatoes are cooked through. Season to taste with sea salt and fresh ground pepper, and garnish with the chopped fresh herbs and reserved orange zest.

SAPPHIRE HILL WINERY

This recipe is our spin on the classic Veal Oscar. The beef tenderloin and sautéed spinach topped with crab and béarnaise sauce is so flavorful and buttery that it melts in your mouth. Our Zafira Zinfandel, with its vanilla notes on the finish, make it the perfect companion. Add a fresh garden salad and crusty homemade bread for a fabulous meal.

55 Front Street
Healdsburg, CA 95448
707-431-1888
sapphirehill.com

STEAK SAPPHIRE
with sautéed spinach, crab & béarnaise sauce

chef Jeff Anderson

Pair with Sapphire Hill Zafira Zinfandel

SERVES 4

STEAKS
4 6-ounce filet mignon steaks
salt and pepper to taste
4 tablespoons butter, divided
8 ounces local Dungeness
   crab meat, diced
8 ounces fresh spinach
   leaves
1 clove garlic, minced
½ teaspoon ground nutmeg
1 teaspoon lemon juice

BÉARNAISE
¼ cup white wine vinegar
¼ cup Sapphire Hill
   Chardonnay
1 tablespoon shallots, minced
1 teaspoon fresh tarragon,
   minced
salt and pepper to taste
3 egg yolks
½ cup melted butter, hot

Preheat a grill for both direct and indirect cooking.

Season the steaks on both sides with salt and pepper and set them aside. In a small saucepan, melt 2 tablespoons of the butter and add the crab meat. Warm the mixture over low heat, stirring occasionally.

In a medium saucepan, add the spinach leaves to salted boiling water and cook for 3 or 4 minutes, until the spinach is soft. Drain the liquid from the pot, and add to the spinach the remaining 2 tablespoons of butter, garlic, nutmeg and lemon juice. Toss to combine. Cover the pan and keep the spinach warm.

Sear the steaks over direct heat for 3 to 5 minutes per side, then move them to indirect heat for an additional 5 to 8 minutes. Remove the steaks from the grill and let them rest.

While the meat rests, prepare the béarnaise sauce by combining the vinegar, wine, shallots, tarragon, salt and pepper in a small saucepan. Bring the mixture to a boil over medium-high heat until it's reduced to about 2 tablespoons. Strain the liquid.

In a double boiler, whisk the egg yolks into the vinegar-wine reduction and continue to whisk over simmering water until the mixture thickens. Remove the top pot from the heat and slowly pour the hot butter into the egg yolk mixture, whisking continually until the butter is fully incorporated. The mixture will become thick and creamy, and is ready to serve immediately.

To assemble the dish, place each steak on a plate, top with the sautéed spinach and then the crab meat. Spoon the béarnaise over the top and serve.

SELBY WINERY

In 2005 my house in Mississippi was blown away during Hurricane Katrina. The company I worked for sent me to New Hampshire to open a complex at a thoroughbred racetrack. Everyone wanted me to do a Gulf Coast dish with local ingredients for the Breeders Cup race, so I chose jambalaya, using lobster instead of crawfish. For "A Wine & Food Affair," I've given jambalaya a Sonoma twist.

215 Center Street
Healdsburg, CA 95448
707-431-1288
selbywinery.com

CREOLE LOBSTER

chef Jimmy Joiner, Covington, Louisiana

Pair with Selby Russian River Valley Syrah

SERVES 8

4 ounces smoked sausage,
  sliced ¼-inch thick
1 cup onions, ½-inch dice
½ cup celery, ½-inch dice
½ cup bell pepper, ½-inch dice
4 ounces baby portobello
  mushrooms, quartered
1 teaspoon fresh garlic, chopped
1 can (14 ounces) fire-roasted
  tomatoes
1 tablespoon lobster base
½ teaspoon dried basil
1-½ teaspoons light brown sugar
1 teaspoon black pepper
1 tablespoon truffle paste
1 pint water
4 cups rice, cooked
1 teaspoon Creole seasoning
4 ounces seared chicken, cut
  into strips
6 ounces cooked shrimp
4 ounces cooked lobster meat,
  cut into chunks
1 tablespoon Italian parsley,
  chopped
1 tablespoon green onions,
  chopped

In a skillet, sauté the sausage to render the fat, about 3 minutes. Add the onions, celery, bell pepper, mushrooms and garlic to the pan and cook for about 5 minutes, until the vegetables are tender.

Add the canned tomatoes, lobster base, basil, brown sugar, black pepper and truffle paste. Stir to combine the ingredients and simmer the mixture for 10 minutes.

Add the water and bring the mixture back to a simmer. Add the cooked rice and simmer 5 minutes more. Add the Creole seasoning, chicken, shrimp and lobster meat. Simmer for 10 minutes. Stir in the parsley and green onions and serve.

SIMI WINERY

Short ribs are incredibly good, virtually impossible to mess up, and accompany Simi Petite Sirah perfectly!

16275 Healdsburg Avenue
Healdsburg, CA 95448
707-433-6981
simiwinery.com

PETITE RIBS
& celeriac puree

chef Kolin Vazzoler

Pair with Simi Winery Dry Creek Valley Petite Sirah

SERVES 6

RIBS

6 bone-in short ribs (about 5-3/4 pounds)

kosher salt

extra-virgin olive oil

1 shallot, cut into 1/2-inch pieces

2 ribs celery, cut into 1/2-inch pieces

2 carrots, peeled and cut into 1/2-inch pieces

2 cloves garlic, smashed

2 to 3 cups Petite Sirah

2 cups beef stock

6 sprigs fresh thyme

2 bay leaves

CELERIAC PUREE

3 heads celeriac (celery root), 2-1/2 to 3 pounds

1 tablespoon olive oil

4 garlic cloves, peeled and sliced

1 teaspoon kosher salt

1/4 teaspoon freshly ground black pepper

5 cups vegetable stock

2 tablespoons unsalted butter

1/4 cup heavy cream

Season each rib generously with salt. Coat an oven-proof pot large enough to accommodate the meat and vegetables with olive oil and bring the oil to high heat. Add the short ribs individually and brown each well, 2 to 3 minutes per side. Set the ribs aside.

Preheat the oven to 375°.

Drain the fat from the pan used to brown the ribs. Add fresh oil to the pan and then the shallots, celery, carrots and garlic. Season the vegetables generously with salt and cook them until they're golden brown, 5 to 7 minutes. Add the wine and scrape the bottom of the pan to dislodge the crispy bits, and reduce the mixture by 1/2.

Return the ribs to the pan and add the beef stock until it just covers the meat. Add the thyme and bay leaves. Cover the pan and place it in the oven for 3 hours. Check periodically and add more stock if the ribs look dry. Turn the ribs over halfway through the cooking process. Remove the lid during the last 20 minutes to let the sauce reduce. The meat should be very tender but not falling apart.

To prepare the celeriac puree, cut off the bottoms and tops of the celery root, peel the remainder, and rinse well with water. Cut the root into 1/2-inch dice. In a 4-quart saucepan, heat the olive oil over low heat until it shimmers. Add the diced celeriac, garlic, salt and pepper and cook until the celeriac begins to soften, approximately 5 minutes. Increase the heat to medium-high and add the stock.

Bring the mixture to a boil and cook until the celeriac is tender and easily pierced with a fork, approximately 15 minutes. Drain the celeriac and place it in a blender, with the butter and cream. Puree the mixture until no lumps are present, and serve with the short ribs and braising liquid.

SUNCE WINERY

Frane's mom, Maria, who still lives in her native village of Sucuraj, prepares Bakalar for special occasions, such as when her sons visit. On the Dalmatian Coast, celebratory dinners almost always include Bakalar, a simple stew of dried cod and potatoes. Cod isn't found in the Adriatic Sea, so it's imported to Croatia in its salted and dried form from cold-water locales.

1839 Olivet Road
Santa Rosa, CA 95401
707-526-9463
suncewinery.com

frane's mom's

BAKALAR
(cod stew & potatoes)

chef Denise Stewart

Pair with Sunce Zora's Vineyard Russian River Valley Pinot Noir

SERVES 6

1 pound dried salt cod
8 ounces olive oil
salt and pepper to taste
1 bay leaf
8 slices lemon, peel removed
8 ounces white onion, diced
4 green onions, chopped
4 garlic cloves, chopped
4 ounces fresh parsley,
    roughly chopped
1 cup Sunce Malvasia Bianca
2 pounds peeled red or
    purple potatoes, quartered
3 large yellow carrots,
    chopped

Wash the salt cod well and soak it in water overnight.

The next day, wash the fish again, then cover it with fresh water in a large pot and add 2 tablespoons of the oil, the salt, pepper, bay leaf and lemon slices, and cook on a low flame until the fish is tender but not falling apart, about 5 to 6 hours.

Remove the cod and reserve the water. Place the cod on a clean cutting board and remove the bones, taking care to keep the fish in large pieces. Briefly sauté the onions, garlic and parsley in olive oil in the cooking pot, then add the wine and cook until the alcohol evaporates, approximately 3 to 5 minutes.

Add the potatoes and carrots and stir. Add the reserved cooking water and simmer the potatoes and carrots until they're tender, then return the cod to the pot. Simmer slowly for an additional 20 to 30 minutes without stirring. Season with salt and pepper to taste and drizzle with more olive oil if desired. Serve with freshly baked bread for dipping into the broth.

TAFT STREET WINERY

Mike Tierney played around with this recipe for a few months before perfecting it to serve at Taft Street's 30th anniversary party. Friends and family gathered at the winery to celebrate our longevity in this crazy business and break in our new bocce court. Mike's Sriracha Chicken paired fabulously with our Sauvignon Blanc.

2030 Barlow Lane
Sebastopol, CA 95472
707-823-2049
taftstreetwinery.com

SRIRACHA CHICKEN

chef Mike Tierney

Pair with Taft Street Russian River Valley Sauvignon Blanc

SERVES 6

¼ cup sriracha sauce
½ stick butter
2 tablespoons cider vinegar
1 tablespoon minced garlic
1 4- to 5-pound chicken
2 tablespoons corn oil
salt and pepper

Preheat the oven to 375°.

Combine the sriracha sauce, butter, vinegar and garlic in a medium bowl and set aside.

Cut the chicken into 16 to 18 pieces: wings split, thighs cut in 1/2 and each 1/2 breast cut into 3 to 4 pieces. Place the chicken pieces in a large roasting pan coated with corn oil, and season with salt and pepper.

Roast for the chicken for 20 minutes, then turn the pieces over, basting them in the pan juices, and pour off the accumulated fat. Continue to cook the chicken for 15 minutes.

Increase the oven temperature to 450°. Remove the chicken from the oven and toss the pieces in the srircha mixture. Return the chicken to the oven and cook 10 minutes. Serve the chicken hot or at room temperature.

THE WINEYARD

Chris O'Connell discovered his passion (and talent) for cooking after joining the wine industry in 2007. He often has company to his house, just to have an excuse to fire up the grill and work on recipes. This particular dish was created in 2010 for a houseful of hungry guests. With various wines on the table, they kept going to back to Syrah, and that's when Chris knew he had the perfect pairing for these sliders.

1305-A Cleveland Avenue
Santa Rosa, CA 95401
707-595-1488
santarosawineyard.com

smokin'

PULLED PORK SLIDERS

with cider vinegar sauce

chef Chris O'Connell

Pair with Santa Rosa Junior College Shone Farm Winery Russian River Valley Syrah

SERVES 10-12

PORK

3 tablespoons paprika

2 tablespoons chili powder

3 tablespoons dark brown sugar

2 tablespoons ground cumin

1 tablespoon kosher salt

1 tablespoon black pepper

1 tablespoon steak seasoning

1 teaspoon cinnamon

1 boneless pork shoulder roast,
   5 to 6 pounds

wood chips – preferably apple
   or cherry

24 small hamburger buns

CIDER VINEGAR SAUCE

1 cup cider vinegar

3 tablespoons dark brown
   sugar

1 teaspoon hot sauce

2 teaspoons kosher salt

½ teaspoon black pepper

½ teaspoon cinnamon

Prepare the pork by blending the paprika, chili powder, brown sugar, cumin, kosher salt, black pepper, steak seasoning and cinnamon in a bowl. Rub the mixture into the meat and place it in the refrigerator for 4 hours or overnight. Remove the seasoned pork from the refrigerator 30 minutes prior to grilling.

In a Weber-type grill, prepare two banks of coals and heat the grill to between 250 and 300° (indirect low heat). Soak the wood chips for 30 minutes while the coals heat. Place the pork shoulder fat side up in the center of the grill and cook it for 8 to 9 hours, adding coals as needed to maintain the temperature. Cook the meat until it reaches an internal temperature of 190°. Every hour or so, add a small handful of wood chips to the fire.

Let the pork rest, covered, for 20 to 30 minutes.

While the meat rests, prepare the cider vinegar sauce. Combine all the ingredients in a saucepan and cook over medium-high heat, until the mixture comes to a boil. Reduce the heat to low and continue to cook the sauce for approximately 15 minutes, or until it has reduced by 1/3.

Transfer the rested pork to a large dish and pull the meat apart with forks. Place a generous spoonful of pork on the bottom of a hamburger bun, pour the sauce over the meat, and add the top half of the bun. Enjoy!

THUMBPRINT CELLARS

Owners Erica and Scott Lindstrom-Dake have been vegetarians for many years, but it wasn't always that way. Erica has been a vegetarian for more than 25 years, and when she and Scott started dating, she told him she wouldn't kiss him if he continued to eat meat. Scott immediately became a vegetarian, and they're still kissing today.

102 Matheson Street
Healdsburg, CA 95448
707-433-2393
thumbprintcellars.com

kissable

BAKED POLENTA

with pinot noir-braised wild mushrooms

chef Erica Lindstrom-Dake

vegi

Pair with Thumbprint Cellars Nugent Vineyard Russian River Valley Pinot Noir

SERVES 4

4-1/2 cups water

1-1/2 teaspoons salt

1-1/2 cups coarse or medium
cornmeal

3 tablespoons olive oil

3/4 teaspoon dried sage

7 tablespoons grated
Parmesan cheese

2 tablespoons butter

1-1/2 pounds mixed wild
mushrooms (chanterelle,
porcini, shiitake), sliced thin

1/4 teaspoon freshly ground
black pepper

6 ounces fontina cheese,
grated

1 cup Thumbprint Nugent
Vineyard Pinot Noir

Preheat the oven to 350°.

In a medium saucepan, bring the water and 1 teaspoon of the salt to a boil. Add the cornmeal in a slow stream, whisking constantly. Whisk in 1 tablespoon of the oil and 1/4 teaspoon of the sage. Reduce the heat and simmer, stirring frequently with a wooden spoon, until the cornmeal is very thick, about 20 minutes. Stir in 3 tablespoons of the Parmesan cheese.

Meanwhile, butter an 8-inch by 12-inch baking dish. In a large frying pan, melt 1 tablespoon of the butter with 1 tablespoon of the oil over moderately high heat. Add 1/2 of the mushrooms, 1/4 teaspoon each of the salt and sage, 1/8 teaspoon of the pepper and 1/2 cup of Pinot Noir. Cook, stirring frequently, until the mushrooms are golden, about 5 minutes. Remove the batch from the pan and repeat with the remaining mushrooms, 1 tablespoon each butter and oil, 1/4 teaspoon each salt and sage, 1/8 teaspoon pepper and 1/2 cup of wine.

Pour half of the polenta into the buttered baking dish and spread it in an even layer. Top with 1/2 of the mushrooms, followed by 1/2 of the fontina and 2 tablespoons of the Parmesan. Repeat with the remaining polenta, mushrooms, fontina and Parmesan.

Bake until the cheese is bubbling, about 15 minutes.

TRIONE VINEYARDS

The Trione team enjoyed this dish at a celebratory dinner after we learned that our 2007 Block 21 Cabernet Sauvignon was awarded 94 points from Wine Enthusiast magazine, and won the Best of Class award at the San Francisco Chronicle Wine Competition. Serve this at your next big celebration; be sure to start it one day ahead.

19550 Geyserville Avenue
Geyserville, CA 95441
707-814-8100
trionewinery.com

cabernet-braised
SHORT RIBS

chef Tim Vallery, Peloton Catering

Pair with Trione Block 21 Alexander Valley Cabernet Sauvignon

SERVES 8

8 short ribs, cut 2 inches thick

kosher salt and freshly ground black pepper to taste

3 tablespoons olive oil

2 yellow onions, peeled, trimmed and split

2 carrots, peeled and cut into $1/2$-inch wheels

2 celery ribs, peeled and cut into 1-inch lengths

12 cloves garlic, peeled

6 sprigs flat-leaf parsley

2 bay leaves

1 bunch fresh thyme

2 tablespoons tomato paste

2 bottles Trione Cabernet Sauvignon

2 quarts beef broth

Preheat the oven to 400°.

Generously season the short ribs with salt and pepper. In a heavy, oven-proof pot, add the oil and heat it to medium-high. Add the ribs and brown them completely, then set them aside.

Reduce the heat and add the onions, carrots, celery, garlic, parsley, bay leaves and thyme, and brown them for 7 to 10 minutes. Add the tomato paste and cook for an additional 2 to 3 minutes, stirring constantly.

Deglaze the pot with the wine and cook to reduce the liquid by 1/2. Add the beef broth, cover the pot tightly and place it in the oven, braising until the meat is fork-tender, approximately 2 hours. Let the mixture cool and place it in the refrigerator overnight.

The following day, warm the mixture over low heat and remove the meat. Reduce the liquid to a saucy consistency and strain it through a fine-mesh strainer. Check for seasoning with salt and pepper, and serve the sauce over the ribs.

TRUETT HURST WINERY

The secret to this recipe is roasting the pork and beef ribs before slowly braising them. The extended simmering of the bones creates an incredibly unctuous, deeply flavored sauce. Finishing the dish with a dollop of ricotta, basil and cherry tomato coulis adds freshness.

5610 Dry Creek Road
Healdsburg, CA 95448
707-433-9545
truetthurst.com

rockin' rattler
PORK & BEEF SUGO
over polenta

chef Peter Brown, Jimtown Store

Pair with Truett Hurst Rattler Rock Zinfandel

SERVES 6-8

RIBS
2 pounds pork spareribs
2 pounds beef back ribs
salt and pepper
3 tablespoons olive oil
1 cup onion, diced
1 cup celery, diced
1 cup carrot, diced
5 whole garlic cloves, peeled
2 bay leaves
1-$\frac{1}{2}$ cups Rattler Rock Zinfandel
3 cups crushed or peeled diced tomatoes
3 cups beef or chicken stock
1 tablespoon fresh sage, chopped
1 tablespoon fresh rosemary, chopped
1 tablespoon fresh thyme, chopped

POLENTA
2-$\frac{1}{2}$ cups whole milk
2-$\frac{1}{2}$ cups water
1 sprig fresh sage
pinch of salt and pepper
1 cup polenta
$\frac{1}{3}$ cup butter, sliced thin

COULIS
2 cups cherry tomatoes
3 cloves garlic
5 tablespoons olive oil
$\frac{1}{2}$ teaspoon salt
$\frac{1}{4}$ teaspoon pepper
2 teaspoons thyme leaves, chopped
1 cup best-quality ricotta, for finishing
basil, chopped, for finishing

Preheat the oven to 350°.

Season the ribs generously with salt and pepper. Place them on a rack and roast them for 1 hour, or until they're well browned.

In a large pot, sauté the onion, celery, carrot and garlic in the olive oil until they're lightly browned. Add the bay leaves and Zinfandel and boil the mixture until almost no liquid remains. Add the tomatoes, stock and roasted ribs, and return the mixture to a boil. Add the herbs, lower the heat to simmer, partially cover, and simmer for 4 hours.

Carefully remove the ribs and allow them to cool until they can be handled. Remove the meat from the ribs and break it into chunks; return the meat to the sauce and discard the bones.

To prepare the polenta, bring the milk, water, sage, salt and pepper to a boil in a large saucepan. Whisk in the polenta and return the mixture to a boil, then lower to a low simmer. Whisk the polenta for 5 minutes, then place the butter on the surface of the polenta and simmer on low, without stirring, for 1 hour.

While the polenta cooks, prepare the coulis by preheating the oven to 450°. Toss in a mixing bowl the tomatoes, garlic, 2 tablespoons of the olive oil, salt and pepper, and scatter them on a baking sheet. Place the sheet pan in the oven for 12 minutes. Place the roasted ingredients in a blender with the thyme and puree, drizzling in the the remaining olive oil. Strain the puree through a sieve and keep it in a warm place.

To serve, put a scoop of polenta on a plate and top it with a cup of the meat sauce. Top with a dollop of ricotta and drizzle the coulis over the top. Finish with a sprinkle of chopped basil.

VML WINERY

After serving the locals in my Oakland restaurant, I decided to relocate to the breathtaking Russian River Valley. While establishing my roots in Sonoma County, I had the pleasure of cooking at VML special events. This was such a pleasant transition for me, given the lively urban grind that I was accustomed to in Oakland. This dish follows the VML philosophy — keep it simple!

4035 Westside Road
Healdsburg, CA 95448
707-431-4404
vmlwine.com

mesquite-charred
BISTRO STEAK
with zinfandel reduction & onion-arugula pilaf

chef Jon Di Bartolo

Pair with VML Bradford Mountain Grist Vineyard Zinfandel

SERVES 6-8

ZINFANDEL REDUCTION
splash extra-virgin olive oil
2 shallots, finely chopped
2 cups VML Bradford Mountain
  Grist Vineyard Zinfandel
1-1/2 cups beef or chicken stock
2 tablespoons freshly ground
  black peppercorns (or 1
  tablespoon coarse-ground
  black pepper)
2 tablespoons butter
kosher salt

STEAKS
3-1/2 to 4 pounds skirt or
  hanger steak
splash extra-virgin olive oil
kosher salt and black pepper

PILAF
splash extra-virgin olive oil
1 medium yellow onion, diced
1 tablespoon butter
2 cups long-grain brown rice
2 cups chicken stock
1/2 teaspoon kosher salt
pinch black pepper
8 to 12 ounces arugula, washed
  and drained

To prepare the reduction sauce, preheat a heavy-gauge saucepan over medium heat. Finely chop the shallots, then add a splash of olive oil and the shallots to the pan. Sauté until the shallots are lightly caramelized, then add the Zinfandel, stock and black pepper, and reduce over medium heat to slightly less than 1/2 of the mixture. Add the butter and turn down the heat to a low simmer.

Prepare a grill using mesquite hardwood. Rinse the steaks, pat them dry and lightly coat them with extra-virgin olive oil. Lightly sprinkle the meat with kosher salt and black pepper, and set it aside for 30 minutes.

Next, prepare the pilaf. Preheat a heavy-gauge, 4-quart saucepan over medium-high heat. Add a healthy splash of olive oil to the pan, followed by the onions and butter. Caramelize the onions, stirring frequently, until they're golden brown. Add the rice and lightly toast it, stirring with a wooden spoon, until the grains start to brown. Add the stock and bring the rice to a boil. Reduce the heat to a simmer, cover the pan, and cook the rice for 35 to 40 minutes. Season with salt and pepper to taste.

While the rice cooks, light the grill. In a mixing bowl, toss the arugula with extra-virgin olive oil and set it aside.

Skirt/hanger steak is a thin cut, so you need high heat to sear in the juices and break down the fat. Grill the steaks over direct (high) heat and flame of the mesquite for 2-1/2 to 3-1/2 minutes per side, depending on their thickness. Remove the steaks when they are medium-rare and cover them with aluminum foil, so that they rest and continue to cook, for 8 to 10 minutes.

Cut the steaks into 4- to 5-inch strips, slicing against the grain. Place a spoonful of pilaf on each plate, top with the arugula and then the sliced steak. Drizzle the sauce over the steak.

WILLIAMSON WINES

Malbec is a great red-meat wine that is adaptable enough to stand up to spicy Mexican, Cajun, Indian and Italian dishes. We love it with barbecue, chili and sausage, and it works beautifully with this grilled skirt steak and the spicy sauce that goes with it.

134 Matheson Street
Healdsburg, CA 95448
707-433-1500
williamsonwines.com

grilled
SKIRT STEAK
with chimi sauce

chef Dawn Williamson

Pair with Williamson Tango Malbec

SERVES 10

5 pounds skirt steak

salt and pepper for the steak

2 cups fresh cilantro, roughly
   chopped

1 teaspoon freshly ground
   black pepper

1 garlic clove

2 jalapeno peppers, roasted,
   peeled and roughly
   chopped

2 cups fresh parsley, roughly
   chopped

1 tablespoon balsamic vinegar

3 tablespoons Williamson
   Tango Malbec wine

2 tablespoons water

½ cup extra-virgin olive oil

Season the steaks with salt and pepper and allow them to rest for 1 hour.

Meanwhile, prepare the chimi sauce by pureeing all of the remaining ingredients in a blender. Season to taste with salt and set the chimi aside.

Skirt steak needs intense heat, so use a grill or a very hot cast-iron pan. Sear the meat quickly before it cooks all the way through, removing it from the grill when it's medium-rare – about 4 minutes per side. Let the steak rest for 10 minutes.

To serve, slice the steak, first cutting a 4-inch section with the grain. Then, slice each of those sections into thin strips about 1/4-inch thick against the grain. This will ensure that you have the shortest muscle fibers, creating a tender, flavorful steak. Serve with the chimi sauce.

WINDSOR OAKS VINEYARDS

Windsor Oaks and chef Les Goodman share a passion for wine, food, Sonoma County and finding innovative ways to put it all together. When Les tasted our 2008 Pinot Noir, he knew immediately that it would go perfectly with any Asian-inspired dish (another love we share). Start this recipe one day in advance.

10810 Hillview Road
Windsor, CA 95492
707-433-4050
windsoroaksvineyards.com

korean-style braised
SHORT RIB RICE BOWL
with kimchi

chef Les Goodman, D'fina Culinary/Sur la Table

Pair with Windsor Oaks Russian River Valley Pinot Noir

SERVES 6-8

3/4 cup salt

3/4 cup sugar

3/4 cup black pepper

4 pounds boneless short ribs, at least 1 inch thick

sesame oil to taste

2 Asian pears, skin on and chopped

1 sweet onion, chopped

1 cup soy sauce

1/4 cup sake (Junmai style)

2 ounces fresh ginger, chopped

1 cup brown sugar

1/2 cup garlic cloves

1 package jasmine rice

16 ounces prepared kimchi (available in Asian markets)

2 tablespoons toasted sesame seeds

Begin the recipe 1 day ahead by combining the salt, sugar and pepper in a bowl. Rub the mixture over the short ribs, and grill them until they're nicely charred on all sides.

Place the cooked ribs in a deep baking dish and generously coat them with sesame oil. While the ribs cool, puree the Asian pears, onion, soy sauce, sake, ginger, brown sugar and garlic in a blender, and pour the mixture over the ribs. Refrigerate the ribs for 8 to 10 hours or overnight.

The next day, preheat the oven to 350°. Add enough water to the baking dish to cover the ribs, tightly cover them with foil, and braise them in the oven for about 3 hours, or until the meat is fork-tender.

Remove the ribs from the liquid and set them aside. Transfer the braising liquid to a pot and reduce the liquid until it thickens and becomes flavorful.

Cook the rice according to the package directions. Serve the ribs over the rice with kimchi and toasted sesame seeds on top.

DESSERTS

Panettone

Dark Chocolate Dreams with Cranberry Relish

Devil's Zin Cake

Chocolate Cupcakes with Salted Caramel Frosting & Red Wine Drizzle

Chocolate-Dipped Pistachio Biscotto with Artisan Salt

Chocolate Ganache Cupcakes

Smoky Autumn & Bacon Truffles

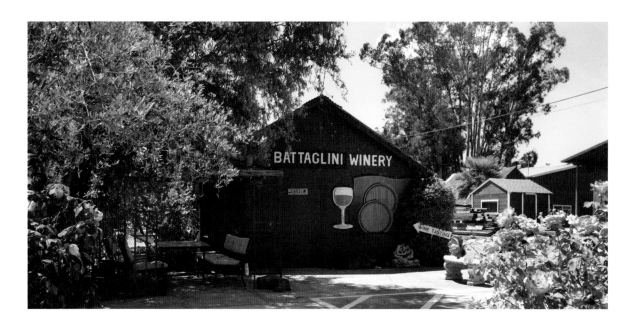

BATTAGLINI ESTATE WINERY

When the children were young, I had to prepare special loaves of panettone without the candied fruit; otherwise, there would have been mounds of fruit left on each plate after the kids picked it out. The adults would eat panettone dipped in wine. The liquor called for in the recipe can be grappa, vermouth, Kahlua, limoncello or any other you like – or mix them together.

2948 Piner Road
Santa Rosa, CA 95401
707-578-4091
battagliniwines.com

PANETTONE
(italian christmas bread)

chef Lucia Battaglini

vegi

Pair with Battaglini Zinfandel

MAKES 3 SMALL LOAVES

3 teaspoons active dry yeast

5 cups flour

1/3 cup milk

3/4 cup butter, room
temperature

6 eggs, room temperature

1 teaspoon vanilla

2 cups sugar

pinch salt

1/4 cup liquor (grappa,
vermouth, limoncello, etc.)

1/2 cup raisins

1/2 cup walnuts, chopped

1/2 cup candied fruit

1/2 cup hazelnuts, chopped

1 egg yolk, for brushing

1 tablespoon milk,
for brushing

One day in advance, mix the yeast and 1 cup of the flour in a bowl. Warm the milk and add it to the yeast and flour. Mix well, cover the bowl and let it stand overnight, or for approximately 10 hours.

The next day, add to this mixture the remaining 4 cups of flour, the butter, eggs, vanilla, sugar, salt and the liquor. Work the dough on a lightly floured surface until it is elastic and no longer sticky. More flour can be added if the dough is too soft, or a bit more milk if the dough is too hard.

Place the dough in a large bowl, cover it with plastic wrap and keep it in a warm place to rise until it doubles in size, approximately 3 to 4 hours. Return the dough to a floured surface and knead it a few times to deflate the air. Return the dough to the bowl, add the raisins, walnuts, candied fruit and hazelnuts, and mix well.

Divide the dough into 3 pieces, and place them on buttered cookie sheets — no more than 2 pieces on the same sheet. In a small bowl, combine 1 egg yolk and 1 tablespoon milk. Brush the tops of the dough lightly with the egg wash. Cut an X on top of each loaf with oiled scissors. Cover the trays and let the dough rise, about 2 hours.

Preheat the oven to 400°.

Place the baking sheet(s) in the preheated oven for 10 minutes, then lower the heat to 375° and bake for 30 minutes more. If the tops get too brown, cover them with foil. Panettones are done when a wooden skewer inserted into the center comes out clean. Cool on a wire rack before serving.

FOPPIANO VINEYARDS

Many people think Petite Sirah only pairs well with grilled or braised red meat – and it certainly does. But with the jammy, ripe fruit and balanced tannins in our Petite Sirah, it matches deliciously with dark chocolate. With one bite of these dark chocolate truffles, you'll think you're dreaming.

12707 Old Redwood Highway
Healdsburg, CA 95448
707-433-7272
foppiano.com

DARK CHOCOLATE DREAMS
with cranberry relish

chef Tim Vallery, Peloton Catering

vegi

Pair with Foppiano Estate Petite Sirah

MAKES 26 1/2-OUNCE TRUFFLES

CRANBERRY RELISH
4 ounces dried cranberries

4 ounces sugar

4 ounces Foppiano Estate
Petite Sirah

TRUFFLES
8 ounces dark chocolate
chips or block, broken
into small pieces

4 ounces heavy cream

1 ounce cranberry relish

1 ounce unsalted butter

7 ounces dark chocolate,
for dipping

8 ounces pistachio nuts,
chopped

First, prepare the cranberry relish (it will keep in the refrigerator for up to 2 months). Combine the cranberries, sugar and Petite Sirah in a stainless steel pot and bring the mixture to a simmer on the stovetop. Simmer for 2 to 3 minutes, then puree the relish in a food processor until it's smooth.

To prepare the truffles, place the 8 ounces of dark chocolate chips or pieces in a medium bowl. Bring the cream to a boil in a small saucepan and pour it over the chocolate, then add the cranberry relish. Stir with a rubber spatula until the mixture is well combined, and let it cool until it firms up. Using a small scoop or melon baller, scoop approximately 1/2 ounce each of the chocolate mixture and roll them into a round ball in the palm of your hand.

Melt the remaining 7 ounces of dark chocolate over a double boiler. Dip each chocolate cranberry ball into the melted chocolate. Using a fork, quickly remove it, letting as much of the melted chocolate drip off as possible. Place the dipped truffles on parchment paper and sprinkle with the chopped pistachios. The dream begins!

MALM CELLARS

This decadent cake gets added richness from our own Malm Cellars Zin Chocolate Sauce, which can be purchased at the winery.

119 W. North Street
Healdsburg, CA 95448
707-364-0441
malmcellars.com

DEVIL'S ZIN CAKE

vegi

chef Amanda Malm

Pair with Malm Cellars North Coast Zinfandel

SERVES 6-8

1 box chocolate cake mix

1 package chocolate instant
  pudding

1 cup sour cream

½ cup lukewarm water

½ cup oil

4 eggs

1 package semisweet
  chocolate chips

Preheat oven to 350°.

Mix the first six ingredients in a large bowl, then fold in the chocolate chips.

Pour the batter into a Bundt pan and bake it for 1 hour. Test for doneness by inserting a toothpick in the center of the cake; when the pick comes out clean, remove the cake from the oven and allow it to cool.

When the cake is cool, flip it onto a plate and drizzle with the Zin Chocolate Sauce and serve.

MEDLOCK AMES

We love using our market gardens and fresh produce as much as we can, but couldn't resist the urge to pair our red Bordeaux-style blend with chocolate! Tim Vallery of Peloton Catering created a chocolate cupcake with salted caramel frosting drizzled with our Medlock Ames Red. These cupcakes also pair well with our Cabernet Sauvignon.

3487 Alexander Valley Road
Healdsburg, CA 95448
707-431-8845
medlockames.com

CHOCOLATE CUPCAKES
with salted caramel frosting & red wine drizzle

vegi

chef Tim Vallery, Peloton Catering

Pair with Medlock Ames Alexander Valley Red

MAKES 24 CUPCAKES

CARAMEL SAUCE
2 ounces sugar
4 ounces heavy cream

CUPCAKES
2 ounces cake flour (weight measure)
2 ounces all-purpose flour
2 ounces cocoa powder
8 egg yolks
1/2 cup granulated sugar
6-1/2 ounces egg whites (liquid measure)
1/4 cup granulated sugar

RED WINE DRIZZLE
1 bottle Medlock Ames Cabernet Sauvignon
1/2 cup granulated sugar

FROSTING
1 pound salted butter
1 pound powdered sugar
4 ounces caramel sauce

First, prepare the caramel sauce. In a stainless steel sauce pot, melt the sugar until it's caramelized. Add the cream and whisk until the ingredients are completely combined. Refrigerate the sauce until it cools.

To prepare the cupcakes, preheat the oven to 325°. In a small bowl, sift the flours and cocoa powder together. In a large bowl, whip the egg yolks and the 1/2 cup of sugar until the yolks are pale.

In a third bowl, whip the egg whites slowly with the remaining 1/4 cup of sugar, until medium peaks form. In 3 batches, fold in the egg whites into the yolks, then the dry ingredients into the yolks. Repeat until all the contents are combined.

Scoop the batter into lined muffin tins, filling each well half-way. Bake in a water bath, until a toothpick comes out clean when inserted into the center of the cupcakes — approximately 20 to 25 minutes.

While the cupcakes bake, prepare the red wine drizzle. In a stainless steel sauce pot, combine the sugar and wine and bring to a simmer. Let the mixture reduce to a syrup, remove the pot from the heat and allow the syrup to cool while you make the frosting.

In a stand mixer, whip the butter with a paddle until it's light and fluffy. Add the powdered sugar. Mix well and then scrape the bowl. In that same bowl, mix in the caramel sauce and whip the mixture until it is well combined.

To assemble the cupcakes, remove them from the muffin tin, apply a generous layer of frosting, and drizzle the red-wine sauce over the top.

PECH MERLE WINERY

We updated this 1894-era family recipe for Pistachio Biscotto by dipping the cookies in rich chocolate and dusting them with artisan salts. They are divine as a dessert, especially when they're dunked in our Cuccio Dry Creek Valley Zinfandel.

4543 Dry Creek Road
Healdsburg CA 95448
707-585-9599
pechmerlewinery.com

chocolate-dipped
PISTACHIO BISCOTTO

vegi

with artisan salt

chef Mama Ruby

Pair with Pech Merle Cuccio Dry Creek Valley Zinfandel

MAKES 36 COOKIES

BISCOTTO
1-3/4 cups flour
1/2 teaspoon baking soda
1/2 teaspoon baking powder
1/8 teaspoon salt
1/2 cup unsalted butter,
  room temperature
1 cup sugar
1-1/2 teaspoons vanilla extract
2 eggs
1-1/2 cups pistachio nuts,
  shelled (salted or unsalted)

CHOCOLATE
8 ounces bittersweet
  chocolate
2 teaspoons vegetable
  shortening
artisan salts of your choice

Sift together the flour, baking soda, baking powder and salt into a bowl and set aside.

Combine the butter, sugar and vanilla in a large bowl, and beat until the mixture is fluffy and light. Mix in the eggs, one at a time, blending well after each addition. Add the pistachios, and then the flour mixture, and mix until just incorporated. Cover the bowl and refrigerate for 1 hour.

Preheat oven to 350°.

Butter and flour a large baking sheet. Divide the biscotto dough in half, and using lightly floured hands, roll each half on a lightly floured surface into a log 1-1/2-inches in diameter. Arrange the logs on the prepared baking sheet, 5 inches apart from each other. Bake for 30 minutes, or until light brown and firm to the touch.

Remove the logs from the oven and let them cool slightly on the baking sheet. Leave the oven on at 350°. Using a spatula, carefully transfer the logs to a flat work surface. Using a serrated knife, cut the logs into diagonal slices 3/4-inch thick. Place the slices, cut side down, on the baking sheet and return it to the oven. Bake for an additional 15 minutes, or until the cookies are golden brown. Transfer them to wire racks to cool.

To prepare the chocolate, combine the bittersweet chocolate and shortening in a double boiler, and melt them over simmering water until the mixture is smooth, stirring occasionally. Remove the chocolate from the heat. Dip one side of the biscotto into the chocolate and place on the baking sheet, chocolate side up. Allow to cool for about 5 minutes, and sparingly sprinkle the salt on top of the chocolate.

ROBERT RUE VINEYARDS

Do you love the seductive combination of Zinfandel and chocolate? We do, and we put the two together in our Robert Rue Chocolate Zinfandel Sauce. It's the star ingredient in these Zinful mini cupcakes.

1406 Wood Road
Santa Rosa, CA 95439
707-578-1601
robertruevineyard.com

chocolate ganache
CUPCAKES

chef Laurie Ferguson

vegi

Pair with Robert Rue Zinfandel

MAKES 48 MINI CUPCAKES

CUPCAKES
1 stick unsalted butter,
  room temperature
1 cup sugar
4 large eggs, room
  temperature
1 jar Robert Rue Chocolate
  Zinfandel Sauce
1 tablespoon vanilla extract
1 cup flour

GANACHE
½ cup heavy cream
8 ounces semisweet
  chocolate chips

Preheat oven to 325°.

Place paper liners a mini muffin pan.

With an electric mixer, cream the butter and sugar in a medium bowl until the mixture is fluffy and light. Add the eggs, 1 at a time. Mix in the chocolate-Zinfandel sauce and vanilla.

Add the flour to the bowl and mix until just combined. Do not over beat; if you do, the cupcakes will be tough. Scoop the batter into the muffin cups and bake the cakes for 12 to 15 minutes, or until they are just set in the middle; you want moist, tender cupcakes.

Let the cakes cool completely. As they do, prepare the ganache by cooking the cream and chocolate chips in the top of a double boiler over simmering water, until the mixture is smooth and warm; stir occasionally.

Spoon a dab of ganache on the top of each cupcake and serve.

WINDSOR VINEYARDS

When Tim Vallery of Peleton Catering prepared four decadent truffles to pair with four of our wines, one truffle in particular left us oohing and aahing over its deliciousness and originality. Hence, the Smoky Autumn & Bacon Truffle was born, inspired by our Russian River Valley Pinot Noir.

308 B Center Street
Healdsburg, CA 95448
707-921-2893
windsorvineyards.com

smoky autumn & bacon
TRUFFLES

chef Tim Vallery, Peloton Catering

Pair with Windsor Vineyards Russian River Valley Pinot Noir

MAKES 21 1/2-OUNCE TRUFFLES

2 ounces bacon, diced, rendered and drained of fat

1 teaspoon whole black peppercorns

2 cloves

1 cinnamon stick

5-1/2 ounces Windsor Vineyards Pinot Noir

2/3 cup heavy cream

6.25 ounces Guittard milk chocolate

1 ounce light corn syrup or invert sugar

1 pound dark chocolate

cocoa powder for garnish

Begin the preparation one day in advance.

Place the rendered bacon in a pot with the black peppercorns, cloves, cinnamon stick and wine. Over medium heat, reduce the liquid to a syrup. Add the cream, turn off the heat and let the mixture steep for 1 hour.

Place the milk chocolate and corn syrup in a mixing bowl. Bring the cream mixture to a boil and then strain it through a fine-mesh sieve over the chocolate. Using a spatula, stir the chocolate and cream until they are well-combined, and refrigerate them overnight.

The next day, use a small scoop or melon baller to scoop 1/2-ounce portions of the mixture onto a parchment paper-lined tray. Using your hands, roll the pieces to make them round, place them back on the parchment and refrigerate until the truffles are set.

Melt the dark chocolate in a double boiler. Dip the truffles into the chocolate with your fingertips and roll them in your palms as before. Roll the truffles in the cocoa powder, making sure to completely cover them.

Allow the truffles to set for at least 30 minutes. Once the chocolate has set, shake off the excess cocoa and serve.

RECIPE INDEX
by winery & lodging

THE WINERIES

57. Acorn Winery/Alegria Vineyards – Duck Chilaquiles with Cherry-Guajillo Chile Sauce
145. Alderbrook Winery – Chicken Ragout with Soft Polenta
147. Alexander Valley Vineyards – Sausage & Mushroom Ragout
119. Amista Vineyards – Risotto Amista
193. Balletto Vineyards & Winery – Rouge et Noir Brie Quiche
257. Battaglini Estate Winery – Panettone
85. Bella Vineyards and Wine Caves – Pumpkin Red Curry
149. Carol Shelton Wines – French Dip Sliders with Karma Au Jus
121. Cellars of Sonoma – Baked Rigatoni with Olives & Sausage
151. Chateau Diana – Mom's Sunday Sauce with Sausages & Meatballs
59. Claypool Cellars – Alligator Sausage Cheesecake with Shrimp
123. Clos du Bois – Spaghetti with Meat Sauce
153. D'Argenzio Winery – Spiedini d' Loiodice con Polenta Enrico
87. Davis Family Vineyards – Harvest Ribollita
155. DeLoach Vineyards – Pollo a la Catalana
157. deLorimier Winery – Roasted Pork Shoulder with Dried Cherry, Bacon & Sweet Onion Compote
125. Draxton Wines – Risotto with Roasted Cippolini, Portobellos & Rainbow Chard
87. Dutcher Crossing Winery – Honey Harvest Tomato Bisque
159. Dutton Estate Winery – Moroccan Lamb Stew with Tart Cherries
259. Foppiano Vineyards – Dark Chocolate Dreams with Cranberry Relish
91. Forchini Vineyards & Winery – Soupe au Pistou
161. Francis Ford Coppola's Winery – Rustic Restaurant Marrakesh Lamb
163. Fritz Underground Winery – Zin-Braised Beef
165. Geyser Peak Winery – St. George & Bacon Grilled Cheese with Caramelized Onions & Herb Aioli
167. Graton Ridge Cellars – Sicilian Lamb Meatballs
61. Gustafson Family Vineyards – Dungeness Crab Salad
93. Hanna Winery – Chris Hanna's Autumn Corn Chowder
95. Hart's Desire Wines – PAG Soup
97. Harvest Moon Estate & Winery – Roasted Apple & Butternut Squash Bisque
63. Hawley Winery – Spicy Crab Arancini
127. Holdredge Wines – Spring Hill Mac & Cheese with Bacon
169. Hook & Ladder Winery – Not So Traditional Osso Buco with Gremolata
65. Hop Kiln Winery – Arancini di Riso
171. Hudson Street Wineries – Lip-Smackin' Baby Back Ribs
129. Inspiration Vineyards – Lemon Risotto
99. J. Keverson Winery – Zin-Marinated Pork & Apple Chili

RECIPE INDEX
by winery & lodging

THE WINERIES continued

173. J. Rickards Winery – Chicken Marbella
175. Kachina Vineyards – Cuban Pork Stew with Sweet Potato Mash
 67. Kelley and Young Wines – Kathleen's Sweet & Spicy Grilled Prawns
177. Kendall-Jackson Healdsburg – Red Wine-Braised Short Ribs with Truffled Celery Root Puree
179. Kendall-Jackson Wine Center – Kobe Tri-Tip Sandwiches with Cabernet-Braised Cabbage & Blue Cheese-Buttermilk Dressing
181. Kokomo Winery – Osso Buco Stew with Gremolata & Freeze-Dried Corn
 69. Korbel Champagne Cellars – Point Reyes Blue Cheese Paté
183. Krutz Family Winery – Sausage Skewers with Mushrooms & Syrah Dipping Sauce
101. La Crema Tasting Room – Chanterelle Soup with Turkey & Cranberry Garnish
185. La Crema Winery – Coq au Vin
187. Limerick Lane Cellars – Wild Boar Sausage
189. Locals Tasting Room – Oxtail & Short Rib Ragu over Soft Polenta
191. Longboard Vineyards – Soul Surfer Ribs
193. Lost Canyon Winery – It's Just Pork … and Chutney
195. Lynmar Estate – Turkey & White Bean Chili
261. Malm Cellars – Devil's Zin Cake
197. Manzanita Creek – New Contadina
131. Martin Ray Winery – Mushroom Ragout
199. Martinelli Winery – Wild Game Stew
201. Matrix Winery – Duck & Pork Cassoulet
203. Mazzocco Sonoma – Beef Ribs with Zinfandel-Maple Reduction Sauce
263. Medlock Ames – Chocolate Cupcakes with Salted Caramel Frosting & Red Wine Drizzle
205. Merriam Vineyards – Josh Silvers' Drunken Duck
207. Mill Creek Vineyards – Nonna's Italian Meatballs
209. Moshin Vineyards – Roast Duck Bread Pudding
211. Mueller Winery – Duck Confit with Emily's Cuvée Reduction & Creamy Polenta
103. Murphy Goode Winery – Posole
213. Old World Winery – Meatloaf with Pancetta & Shiitake Mushrooms
215. Papapietro Perry Winery – Pancetta & Bacon Pot Pie
105. Paradise Ridge Winery – Mushroom & Brie Soup with Truffle Oil
265. Pech Merle Winery – Chocolate-Dipped Pistachio Biscotto with Artisan Salt
217. Pedroncelli Winery – Chicken & Sausage Jambalaya
133. Portalupi Winery – Cannelloni con Spinaci e Salmone
 71. Quivira Vineyards and Winery – Zinfandel-Braised Pork with Vella Dry Jack Polenta
219. Ridge Vineyards/Lytton Springs – Ricotta Malfatti with Sweet Italian Sausage, Spinach & Peppers

RECIPE INDEX
by winery & lodging

THE WINERIES continued

221. Roadhouse Winery – Margherita Pizza
267. Robert Rue Vineyard – Chocolate Ganache Cupcakes
223. Robert Young Estate Winery – South African-Style Boerewors Sausages with Merlot-Caramelized Onions
73. Rodney Strong Vineyards – Red, Smoked & Blue Filet Mignon
225. Route 128 Vineyards & Winery – Braised Pork Shank with Apricots
227. Rued Vineyards – Spinach & Portobello Mushroom Lasagne
229. Russian Hill Estate Winery – Provencal Lamb Daube with Red Wine, Olives & Oranges
113. Russian River Vineyards – Seared Pork Tenderloin with Rocket-Chicory Salad
231. Sapphire Hill Winery – Steak Sapphire with Sautéed Spinach, Crab & Béarnaise Sauce
75. Sbragia Family Winery – Bruschetta with Mushroom Pesto
233. Selby Winery – Lobster Creole
77. Sheldon Wines – Wood Stove Fondue with Tri-Color Potatoes
235. Simi Winery – Petite Ribs & Celariac Puree
135. Soda Rock Winery – Peppery Pancetta Pasta
237. Sunce Winery – Frane's Mom's Bakalar
239. Taft Street Winery – Sriracha Chicken
241. The Wineyard – Smokin' Pulled Pork Sliders with Cider Vinegar Sauce
243. Thumbprint Cellars – Kissable Baked Polenta with Pinot Noir-Braised Wild Mushrooms
107. Toad Hollow Vineyards – Mushroom-Leek Zuppa
115. Topel Winery – 'Baked Comfort' Tomato Bread Pudding
79. Trentadue Winery – Costeaux French Bakery Focaccia
245. Trione Winery – Cabernet-Braised Short Ribs
247. Truett Hurst Winery – Rockin' Rattler Pork & Beef Sugo over Polenta
137. Twomey Cellars – Risotto al Radicchio Rosso
249. VML Winery – Mesquite-Charred Bistro Steak with Zinfandel Reduction & Onion-Arugula Pilaf
81. West Wines – Swedish Gravlax with Mustard Sauce
139. White Oak Vineyards & Winery – Bill's Bolognese
251. Williamson Wines – Grilled Skirt Steak with Chimi Sauce
141. Wilson Winery – Diane's Baked Penne Pasta
253. Windsor Oaks Vineyards & Winery – Korean-Style Braised Short Rib Rice Bowl with Kimchi
269. Windsor Vineyards – Smoky Autumn & Bacon Truffles

RECIPE INDEX
by winery & lodging

THE LODGINGS

3. Applewood Inn & Restaurant – Applewood's White Gazpacho

5. Avalon Luxury Bed & Breakfast – Eggs Florentine with Hollandaise Sauce

7. Bella Villa Messina – Spinach Fritatta

9. Belle du Jour Inn – Cheese Soufflés

11. Camellia Inn – Italian Brunch Asparagus

13. Case Ranch Inn – Baked Pears with Granola

15. Creekside Inn & Resort – Roasted Pepper & Pea Tortilla

17. Dawn Ranch Lodge – Crispy Pork Belly Sandwich

19. English Tea Garden Bed & Breakfast – Potato, Cheddar & Mushroom Egg Bake

21. Farmhouse Inn & Restaurant – Pumpkin Waffles with Apple Cider Sauce

23. Fern Grove Cottages – Maple & Fruit Bread

25. Hampton Inn & Suites – Oatmeal-Blueberry Pancakes

27. Healdsburg Country Gardens – Melon Delight with Honey-Lime Sauce

29. Highlands Resort – Orange-Bittersweet Chocolate Muffins

31. Honor Mansion – Santa Fe Bake with Sun-Dried Tomato Sauce

33. Hope-Merrill House – Baked Cheese Omelet

35. Inn at Occidental – Orange Cream-Filled French Toast with Orange Sauce

37. Old Crocker Inn – Nut-Crusted French Toast

39. The Raford Inn Bed and Breakfast – Morning Glorious Muffins

41. Rio Villa Beach Resort – Aunt Wanda's Okie Doughs

43. Santa Nella House Bed and Breakfast – Mexican Cornbread

45. Sonoma Orchid Inn – Potato & Asparagus Tart

47. Village Inn & Restaurant – Mushroom Bisque

49. Vine Hill Inn Bed and Breakfast – Spinach Fritatta

51. Vintners Inn/John Ash Restaurant – Liberty Duck Confit Hash Cakes

53. West Sonoma Inn & Spa – Spicy Scrambled Eggs

Thank YOU!...

The members of the Wine Road would like to extend a thank-you to the guests that travel near and far, year after year to visit the Wine Road, patronize our wineries and lodgings and spread the word about the beauty that is SONOMA COUNTY.

We wanted to take a minute to share some of our Wine Road highlights with you...

First off, we're pretty excited with the final numbers from our 34th Annual Barrel Tasting, which took place in March of 2012.

BARREL TASTING

- 20,000 guests attended, visiting from 47 states.
- $2.8 million in wine sales in two weekends

Our philosophy ~ shoot it then "pin it"...

We firmly believe a picture is worth a thousands words, so to show you what you're missing when you're not along the Wine Road, we have fun posting photos on our various **Wine Road Northern Sonoma County Pinterest boards** – feel free to repin!

Let your creative juices flow....

If you enjoy talking about your Wine Road adventures and you want the world to read about it, you may enjoy being a guest blogger for us. Shoot an email to **beth@wineroad.com** and we'll see if we can make that happen for you.

If you are simply overwhelmed with the options along the Wine Road, we can help with that too! Just send a note to **tracy@wineroad.com** with your trip details, dates, types of wine you enjoy, reason for the trip (anniversary, birthday, much needed R & R), type of lodging you prefer, and our guest concierge can help you fine-tune your itinerary. Although Tracy cannot book any rooms, events or transportation for you, she can help with all of your planning and answer any travel questions you may have.

There is nothing we like more than hearing from our guests. What are your favorite wineries to visit and where do you like to stay? By all means, share with us on **facebook.com/WineRoad** or our event pages. Your ideas and advice helps others planning their visit.

What's New...

Now in our 36th year, the Wine Road has grown from the original 9 founding winery members to a spirited collection of 190. Along with those world-class wine producers, add 56 lodging properties throughout the Alexander, Dry Creek and Russian River valleys of Northern Sonoma County, truly Heaven Condensed!

Our increased membership is not the only change. We're happy to say we now have a mobile version of our website for our tech-savvy travelers, with a way for you to track your wine recommendations and share with your friends on the fly. Our website even has a way for you to connect with our winery members when they are in your area for a special wine tasting opportunity; look for "Wine Road on the Road." For those times when you're already on the "Road" looking for information, just download our new free app – **WineRoad, for iPhone and Android.**

Wine Road is an easy drive, about an hour north of the Golden Gate Bridge. We enjoy the grandeur of the Pacific Ocean, stately redwoods, picturesque towns and rolling vineyards, all easily accessed along quiet country roads. If you live locally, we hope you enjoy all of these envious amenities right in your backyard.

Save Big – Ticket to the Wine Road...

The Wine Road now offers a great way to save $$ while visiting our member wineries and lodgings: **"Ticket to the Wine Road."**

Log onto wineroad.com and click on the TICKET link to see the list of wineries and lodgings that are participating in the program. You can buy a 1-day pass for $25 or a 3-day pass for $50, then simply select the dates you want to use the pass when you place your order. Currently 80 wineries and 20 lodgings have special offers; complimentary tasting, barrel samples or other fun offers for "Ticket" holders. When you order you will see that event weekends are blackout dates, and the "Ticket" will not work for groups of 6 or more.

Check it out – "Ticket to the Wine Road," then plan your tasting adventure.

So Much To Share...

Don't miss out on Wine Road news. We share our insider news, stories, specials and contests online. We love hearing from you and having a forum where you can share your photos, comments and suggestions with other Wine Road guests. Stay in the loop with **Facebook, Twitter and our weekly blog.**

Save The Date For These Annual Wine Road Events...

Winter WINEland
January - Martin Luther King Jr. Birthday Weekend

Wine Wine Wine, it is all about the WINE. Each of the 100+ wineries will focus on one varietal for the weekend and offer library wines, vertical tastings, new releases or vineyard designated wines. We'll even do our best to create a "winter" feel in our tasting rooms because it is January...although we're usually spoiled with great weather!

Tickets are available online beginning in mid-November.

Barrel Tasting
March - First two weekends

Pack a picnic and join us for this extraordinary tasting opportunity — like the name says, you will be sampling wine directly from the barrel! This is your chance to get into the cellar at over 100 wineries, sample wine from the barrel and talk with winemakers. It's also an opportunity to purchase "futures," often at a discount. Come back to the winery after the wine is bottled (typically 12-16 months later) and pick up your purchase.

Tickets are available online beginning January 1st with "early bird" pricing. Price increases February 1st and again at the door. Advance sales end one week prior to the event.

A Wine & Food Affair
November - The first full weekend

An extraordinary weekend of wine and food pairings, complete with the current volume of "Tasting Along the Wine Road" cookbook and event logo glass. All participating wineries will have a recipe for a favorite dish in the cookbook, which they will prepare both days for you to sample, paired with the perfect wine. Many Wine Road lodgings also provide recipes for inclusion in the cookbook.

Tickets are available online beginning in September. There are no tickets sold at the door for this event.

For details on these annual events and other wine
country events and festivals sponsored by our members, visit
wineroad.com

Feel-Good Moment...

In April 2012, Wine Road Executive Director Beth Costa and President, Bruce Thomas from Mill Creek Winery presented the Redwood Empire Food Bank with a portion of the proceeds from this year's 34th annual Barrel Tasting. More than 140 wineries located in the Dry Creek, Russian River and Alexander valleys threw open their cellar doors to celebrate the 2012 Barrel Tasting, and during the two weekends, raised an impressive $35,000 for the Food Bank.

Bruce Thomas, Wine Road President, Beth Costa, Wine Road Executive Director & David Goodman, REFB Executive Director.

The Redwood Empire Food Bank serves 60,000 people in Sonoma, Mendocino, Lake, Humboldt and Del Norte counties each month, including children, seniors and working families.

"The day we visit the Redwood Empire Food Bank with our donation check is the best day of the year for us. The Wine Road Board of Directors, staff and members are just so thrilled to be able to help our community in this way. We know our contribution reaches thousands of people."

This year's $35,000 donation was a combination of $22,000 from the Wine Road Barrel Tasting, $6,000 from Wine Road Winter WINEland, $2,000 from our Ticket to the Wine Road and $5,000 from customers who donated when ordering tickets.

OUR AVAs
(AMERICAN VITICULTURAL AREAS)

The mission of Wine Road is to increase awareness of the Alexander,
Dry Creek and Russian River valleys through education and marketing, while
promoting Sonoma County as the year-round wine country destination.

To that end, we've included some general information about the three AVAs that we represent in Northern Sonoma County, California.

Alexander Valley
Total acres: 32,536 • Vineyard acres: 15,000 • Number of wineries: 49, growing 23 grape varieties

This valley is named for the 19th-century pioneer Cyrus Alexander, explorer of Northern Sonoma County and resident of the area. Alexander Valley flanks the Russian River from Cloverdale to Healdsburg. Along the heavily graveled benchlands, one finds world-class Cabernet Sauvignon grapes. Considered one of the most diverse grapegrowing regions in California, the valley is also planted to Chardonnay, Zinfandel, Merlot, Sauvignon Blanc and other varieties, which prosper on the long, undulating valley floor and hillsides.

Forty years ago, prunes and walnuts reigned supreme in the Alexander Valley, and the flatlands were dotted with bovine herds. Today, the lowlands produce Chardonnays that achieve a rich and flavorful ripeness. The warmer northern end of the valley favors Cabernet Sauvignon, Zinfandel, Merlot and newcomers like Syrah and Sangiovese. Vineyards that scale the hillsides surrounding the valley floor provide grapes with deep and complex flavors. Hunt around and you can also still find some of the juiciest, most succulent prunes you've ever tasted.

Dry Creek Valley
Total acres: 78,387 • Vineyard acres: 9,000 • Number of wineries: 60+, growing 26 grape varieties

Dry Creek Valley's history of grape growing and winemaking is among the longest in California, with roots beginning more than 135 years ago. The precise blend of climate, soil and exposure that produces grapes of singular quality and character is the true allure of the region.

Dry Creek Valley is approximately 16 miles long and 2 miles wide. It is framed on the western edge by rugged mountains ridges rimmed with redwoods and evergreens. The climate reflects both coastal and inland influences and is classified as a Region II. The proximity to the ocean is tempered by the intervening coastal hills breached by the Russian River. While DCV experiences coastal cooling in the late afternoon during summer, fog rarely enters the valley until after nightfall. The climate is warmer in the north and cooler in the south, allowing for diversity of grape growing.

Dry Creek Valley is recognized as a premium winegrowing region in California and Zinfandel is the signature varietal. However, the diversity of the soil encourages the production of a broad range of top quality Bordeaux and Mediterranean varietals.

Russian River Valley
Total acres: 126,600 • Vineyard acres: 10,000 • Number of wineries: 130, growing 30 grape varieties

What makes Russian River Valley stand out is its climate. This low-lying flat plain extends south and west of Healdsburg as it winds its way along the Russian River and descends to meet the Pacific at Jenner, then makes it way toward the Golden Gate Bridge, ending about 55 miles north of this landmark. This area thrives from the coastal influences of the Pacific Ocean, which makes it an exceptional place for growing cool-climate grapes like Pinot Noir, Chardonnay as well as sparkling wine grapes.

The Russian River Valley is so expansive that it has two smaller appellations within it: Green Valley and Chalk Hill. Green Valley is one of the smallest appellations in the county, nestled in the southwest corner of the Russian River Valley. This area is greatly affected by the cooling coastal elements, which benefit the cool-climate grapes that flourish in these conditions. Chalk Hill, named for the volcanic soil that makes up the area, is a unique little gem known for its outstanding wines. By being situated in the northwest corner of Russian River Valley, it has warmer temperatures that allow Merlot and Cabernet Sauvignon to thrive.

Russian River Valley Chardonnays are exceptional, slightly more lean and refined than those of Alexander Valley, yet the fruit is still developed enough to sustain months in oak barrels, creating depth and complexity. Pinot Noir brought this area international acclaim. Whereas most red wines focus on flavor, Pinot Noir is about an alluring, sensual, velvety mouth-feel. It is a textural delight that can only be found where morning fog turns to warm afternoons, so that grape maturity is achieved without loss of depth and suppleness.

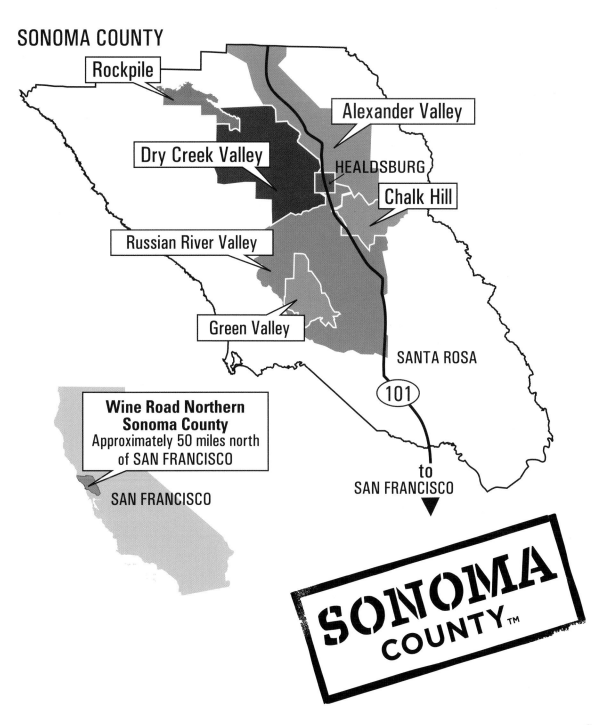

WINE ROAD NORTHERN SONOMA COUNTY

SONOMA COUNTY

Rockpile

Alexander Valley

Dry Creek Valley

HEALDSBURG

Chalk Hill

Russian River Valley

Green Valley

SANTA ROSA

101

Wine Road Northern Sonoma County
Approximately 50 miles north of SAN FRANCISCO

SAN FRANCISCO

to
SAN FRANCISCO

SONOMA COUNTY™